<u>DIABETIC MEAL PREP</u>
FOR BEGINNERS

EFFECTIVE, HEALTHY, AND DELICIOUS RECIPES TO MANAGE DIABETES THE PERFECT DIABETIC COOKBOOK FOR BEGINNERS

© Copyright 2021 - All rights reserved.

Table of Contents

Introduction

What Makes a Good Diet for a Diabetic?

No matter what type of diabetes you have and what your medication, exercise, or long-term healthcare plans are, your ideal diet is actually going to be quite similar to any other diabetic's diet. Starting with nutritional balance, you need to make sure you are eating the right ratio of fat, protein, and carbohydrate. You also need to make sure you are eating the right types of carbohydrates, as there are vast differences between carbohydrates, healthy and unhealthy varieties.

Your carbohydrate needs are actually no different as a diabetic than they were before diabetes. You still need, at most, 50% of your **Calories:** from carbohydrates, which equals 300 g. However, if you are used to eating less, try and eat less. Fats are not as harmful as we have been made to believe, and a diet with healthy fats is no problem.

Just be careful if your gallbladder is affected and avoid trans fats. Also, remember, protein can be broken down into glucose, so if you eat a meal high in proteins, you must check your blood sugar one or two hours after eating.

Finally, you need to consider what micronutrients you are getting and what ones you need. Our micronutrients come in four types: vitamins, minerals, antioxidants, and fiber. Make sure to eat a balanced amount of all the necessary vitamins and minerals. Pay special attention to Vitamin D; it regulates hormones and helps you make insulin and chromium, which lowers your blood sugar levels.

When it comes to antioxidants, consider a trans-resveratrol supplement to help your body heal and reduce inflammation. Another suggestion concerns fiber; make sure to eat the recommended amount, and ideally twice the recommended amount. This slows down digestion, preventing blood sugar spikes and hunger.

Foods That Are Good for Diabetics

When you have diabetes, it can feel as though there is nothing you can eat anymore. Rest assured there are plenty of perfectly safe foods if you know where to look. In fact, there are plenty of foods that will improve your symptoms and make your life easier.

- Whole grains.
- Low-carb tubers and roots.
- Fresh, frozen, or raw vegetables.
- Fresh fruit with high-fiber content.
- Fresh berries with a low-sugar content.
- Non-sweet fruits.
- Sugar-free and calorie-free products.
- Freshly boiled beans. Tinned and refried beans are higher in simple carbs.
- Nuts and seeds: dry roasted or raw; walnuts, almonds, pistachios, peanuts.
- Fresh meat.
- Whole dairy.
- Black coffee.

CHAPTER 1:

Breakfast

1. Apple Filled Swedish Pancake

Preparation Time: 25 minutes
Cooking Time: 20 minutes
Servings: 6
Ingredients:

- 2 apples, cored and sliced thin
- ¾ cup egg substitute
- ½ cup fat-free milk
- ½ cup sugar-free caramel sauce
- 1 tbsp. reduced-calorie margarine
- ½ cup flour
- 1–1/2 tbsp. brown sugar substitute
- 2 tsps. water
- ¼ tsp. cinnamon
- 1/8 tsp. cloves
- 1/8 tsp. salt
- Non-stick cooking spray

Directions:

1. Heat the oven to 400°F. Place the margarine in the cast iron or oven-proof skillet, and place it in the oven until the margarine is melted.
2. In a medium bowl, whisk together flour, milk, egg substitute, cinnamon, cloves, and salt until smooth.
3. Pour the batter into a hot skillet and bake 20–25 minutes until puffed and golden brown.
4. Spray a medium saucepan with cooking spray. Heat over medium heat.
5. Add apples, brown sugar, and water. Cook, stirring occasionally until apples are tender and golden brown, about 4–6 minutes.
6. Pour the caramel sauce into a microwave-proof measuring glass and heat 30–45 seconds, or until warmed through.
7. To serve, spoon apples into pancake and drizzle with caramel. Cut into wedges.

Nutrition:

- **Calories:** 193
- **Total Carbs:** 25 g
- **Net Carbs:** 23 g
- **Protein:** 6 g Fat 2 g
- **Sugar:** 12 g
- **Fiber:** 2 g

2. Apple Topped French Toast

Preparation Time: 10 minutes
Cooking Time: 10 minutes
Servings: 2
Ingredients:

- 1 apple, peel and sliced thin
- 1 egg
- ¼ cup skim milk
- 2 tbsps. margarine, divided
- 4 slices Healthy Loaf Bread
- 1 tbsp. Splenda® brown sugar
- 1 tsp. vanilla
- ¼ tsp. cinnamon

Directions:

1. Melt 1 tbsp. margarine in a large skillet over med-high heat. Add apples, Splenda®, and cinnamon and cook, stirring frequently, until apples are tender.
2. In a shallow dish, whisk together egg, milk, and vanilla.
3. Melt the remaining margarine in a separate skillet over med-high heat. Dip each slice of bread in the egg mixture and cook until golden brown on both sides.
4. Place two slices of Healthy Loaf Bread on plates and top with apples. Serve immediately.

Nutrition:

- **Calories:** 394
- **Total Carbs:** 27 g
- **Net Carbs:** 22 g
- **Protein:** 10 g
- **Fat:** 23 g
- **Sugar:** 19 g
- **Fiber:** 5 g

3. "Bacon" & Egg Muffins

Preparation Time: 10 minutes
Cooking Time: 15 minutes
Servings: 6
Ingredients:

- 1 ¼ cups frozen hash browns, thawed
- 1 cup egg substitute
- 2 turkey sausage patties, diced
- 2 tbsps. onion, diced fine
- 2 tbsps. turkey bacon, cooked and chopped
- 2 tbsps. Monterey Jack cheese, grated
- 1 tbsp. fat-free sour cream
- 1 garlic clove, diced fine
- 1 tsp. vegetable oil
- ¼ tsp. salt
- 1/8 tsp. black pepper
- Cooking spray

Directions:

1. Heat the oven to 400°F. Spray a 6-cup muffin pan with cooking spray.
2. Divide the hash browns evenly among the muffin cups, pressing firmly on the bottoms and up the sides.
3. In a large skillet, over medium heat, heat oil until hot. Add onion, and cook, stirring frequently until tender.
4. Add garlic and sausage and cook for one minute.
5. Remove the skillet from heat and stir in sour cream.
6. In a medium bowl, beat egg substitute with salt and pepper. Pour egg mixture evenly over the hash browns.
7. Top with sausage mixture, bacon, and cheese. Bake 15–18 minutes, or until the eggs are set. Serve immediately.

Nutrition:

- **Calories:** 165
- **Total Carbs:** 13 g
- **Net Carbs:** 12 g
- **Protein:** 11 g
- **Fat:** 7 g
- **Sugar:** 1 g
- **Fiber:** 1 g

4. Blueberry Cinnamon Muffins

Preparation Time: 10 minutes
Cooking Time: 30 minutes
Servings: 10
Ingredients:

- 3 eggs
- 1 cup blueberries
- 1/3 cup half-n-half
- ¼ cup margarine, melted
- 1½ cup almond flour
- ⅓ cup Splenda®
- 1 tsp. baking powder
- 1 tsp. cinnamon

Directions:

1. Heat the oven to 350°F. Line 10 muffin cups with paper liners.
2. In a large mixing bowl, combine dry ingredients.
3. Stir in wet ingredients and mix well.
4. Fold in the blueberries and spoon evenly into the lined muffin pan.
5. Bake 25–30 minutes, or they pass the toothpick test.

Nutrition:

- **Calories:** 194
- **Total Carbs:** 12 g
- **Net Carbs:** 10 g
- **Protein:** 5 g
- **Fat:** 14 g
- **Sugar:** 9 g
- **Fiber:** 2 g

5. Breakfast Pizza

Preparation Time: 10 minutes
Cooking Time: 30 minutes
Servings: 8
Ingredients:

- 12 eggs
- ½ lb. breakfast sausage
- 1 cup bell pepper, sliced
- 1 cup red pepper, sliced
- 1 cup cheddar cheese, grated
- ½ cup half-and-half
- ½ tsp. salt
- ¼ tsp. pepper

Directions:

1. Heat oven to 350°F.
2. In a large cast-iron skillet, brown the sausage. Transfer to a bowl.
3. Add peppers and cook for 3–5 minutes or until they begin to soften. Transfer to a bowl.
4. In a small bowl, whisk together the eggs, cream, salt, and pepper. Pour into the skillet. Cook for 5 minutes or until the sides start to set.
5. Bake for 15 minutes.
6. Remove from the oven and set it to broil. Top "crust" with sausage, peppers, and cheese. Broil 3 minutes, or until cheese is melted and starts to brown.
7. Let rest for 5 minutes before slicing and serving.

Nutrition:

- **Calories:** 230
- **Total Carbs:** 4 g
- **Protein:** 16 g
- **Fat:** 17 g
- **Sugar:** 2 g
- **Fiber:** 0 g

6.   Cafe Mocha Smoothies

Preparation Time: 0 minutes
Cooking Time: 5minutes
Servings: 3
Ingredients:

- 1 avocado, remove pit and cut in half
- 1 ½ cup almond milk, unsweetened
- ½ cup canned coconut milk
- 3 tbsps. Splenda®
- 3 tbsps. unsweetened cocoa powder
- 2 tsps. instant coffee
- 1 tsp. vanilla

Directions:

1. Place everything but the avocado in the blender. Process until smooth.
2. Add the avocado and blend until smooth and no chunks remain.
3. Pour into glasses and serve.

Nutrition:

- **Calories:** 109
- **Total Carbs:** 15 g
- **Protein:** 6 g
- **Fat:** 1 g
- **Sugar:** 13 g
- **Fiber:** 0 g

7. Cauliflower Breakfast Hash

Preparation Time: 10 minutes
Cooking Time: 20 minutes
Servings: 2
Ingredients:

- 4 cups cauliflower, grated
- 1 cup mushrooms, diced
- ¾ cup onion, diced
- 3 bacon slices
- ¼ cup sharp cheddar cheese, grated

Directions:

1. In a medium skillet, over med-high heat, fry the bacon, set it aside.
2. Add vegetables to the skillet and cook, stirring occasionally, until golden brown.
3. Cut bacon into pieces and return to the skillet.
4. Top with cheese and allow it to melt. Serve immediately.

Nutrition:

- **Calories:** 155
- **Total Carbs:** 16 g
- **Net Carbs:** 10 g
- **Protein:** 10 g
- **Fat:** 7 g
- **Sugar:** 7 g
- **Fiber:** 6 g

8.   Cheese Spinach Waffles

Preparation Time: 10 minutes
Cooking Time: 20 minutes
Servings: 4
Ingredients:

- 2 bacon strips, cooked and crumbled
- 2 eggs, lightly beaten
- ½ cup cauliflower, grated
- ½ cup frozen spinach, chopped (squeeze water out first)
- ½ cup low-fat mozzarella cheese, grated
- ½ cup low-fat cheddar cheese, grated
- 1 tbsp. margarine, melted
- ¼ cup reduced-fat Parmesan cheese, grated
- 1 tsp. onion powder
- 1 tsp. garlic powder
- Non-stick cooking spray

Directions:

1. Thaw spinach and squeeze out as much of the water as you can, place in a large bowl.
2. Heat your waffle iron and spray with cooking spray.
3. Add remaining ingredients to the spinach and mix well.
4. Pour small amounts on the waffle iron and cook like you would for regular waffles. Serve warm.

Nutrition:

- **Calories:** 186
- **Total Carbs:** 2 g
- **Protein:** 14 g
- **Fat:** 14 g
- **Sugar:** 1 g
- **Fiber:** 0 g

9. Cinnamon Apple Granola

Preparation Time: 5 minutes
Cooking Time: 35 minutes
Servings: 4
Ingredients:

- 1 apple, peel and diced fine
- ¼ cup margarine, melted
- 1 cup walnuts or pecans
- 1 cup almond flour
- ¾ cup flaked coconut
- ½ cup sunflower seeds
- ½ cup hemp seeds
- 1/3 cup Splenda®
- 2 tsps. cinnamon
- 2 tsps. vanilla
- ½ tsp. salt

Directions:

1. Heat oven to 300°F. Line a large baking sheet with parchment paper.
2. Place the nuts, flour, coconut, seeds, Splenda®, and salt in a food processor. Pulse until mixture resembles coarse crumbs but leave some chunks.
3. Transfer to a bowl and add apple and cinnamon. Stir in margarine and vanilla until well coated, and the mixture starts to clump together.
4. Pour into the prepared pan and spread out evenly. Bake 25 minutes, stirring a couple of times, until it starts to brown.
5. Turn the oven off and let the granola sit inside for 5–10 minutes. Remove from the oven and cool completely; it will crisp up more as it cools. Store in an airtight container.

Nutrition:

- **Calories:** 360
- **Total Carbs:** 19 g
- **Net Carbs:** 14 g
- **Protein:** 10 g
- **Fat:** 28 g
- **Sugar:** 12 g
- **Fiber:** 5 g

10. Cinnamon Rolls

Preparation Time: 15 minutes
Cooking Time: 20 minutes
Servings: 6
Ingredients:

- 4 eggs
- 1 ripe banana
- 2/3 cup coconut flour
- 6 tbsps. honey, divided
- 6 tbsps. coconut oil, soft, divided
- 1 tsp. vanilla
- 1 tsp. baking soda
- ½ tsp. salt
- 1 tbsp. + ½ tsp. cinnamon

Directions:

1. Heat oven to 350°F. Line a cookie sheet with parchment paper.
2. In a medium bowl, lightly beat the eggs. Beat in the banana. Add 2 tbsps. honey, 2 tbsps. melted coconut oil and vanilla and mix to combine.
3. Mix in flour, salt, baking soda, and ½ tsp. cinnamon until thoroughly combined. If the dough is too sticky, add more flour, a little at a time.
4. Line a work surface with parchment paper and place dough on top. Place another sheet of parchment paper on top and roll out into a large rectangle.
5. In a small bowl, combine 2 tbsps. honey, 2 tbsps. coconut oil, and 1 tbsps. of cinnamon and spread on dough.
6. Roll up and cut into 6 equal pieces. Place on prepared pan and bake 15-30 minutes, or until golden brown.
7. Let cool for 10 minutes. Stir together the remaining 2 tbsps. of honey and coconut oil and spread over warm rolls. Serve.

Nutrition:

- **Calories:** 247
- **Total Carbs:** 23 g
- **Protein:** 4 g
- **Fat:** 17 g
- **Sugar:** 20 g
- **Fiber:** 1 g

11. Coconut Breakfast Porridge

Preparation Time: 2 minutes
Cooking Time: 10 minutes
Servings: 4
Ingredients:

- 4 cup vanilla almond milk, unsweetened
- 1 cup unsweetened coconut, grated
- 8 tsps. coconut flour
- Blueberries, for serving (optional)
- Honey, for serving (optional)

Directions:

1. Add the coconut to a saucepan and cook over med-high heat until it is lightly toasted. Be careful not to let it burn.
2. Add milk and bring to a boil. While stirring, slowly add flour, cook, and stir until the mixture starts to thicken for about 5 minutes.
3. Remove from heat; mixture will thicken more as it cools. Ladle into bowls, add blueberries, or drizzle with a little honey if desired.

Nutrition:

- **Calories:** 231
- **Total Carbs:** 21 g
- **Net Carbs:** 8 g
- **Protein:** 6 g
- **Fat:** 14 g
- **Sugar:** 4 g
- **Fiber:** 13 g

12. Cottage Cheese Pancakes

Preparation Time: 5 minutes
Cooking Time: 5 minutes
Servings: 2
Ingredients:

- 1 cup low-fat cottage cheese
- 4 egg whites
- ½ cup oats
- 1 tbsp. Stevia, raw, optional
- 1 tsp. vanilla
- Non-stick cooking spray
- Sugar-free syrup, for serving (optional)
- Fresh berries, for serving (optional)

Directions:

1. Place all ingredients into a blender and process until smooth.
2. Spray a medium skillet with cooking spray and heat over medium heat.
3. Pour about ¼ cup batter into a hot pan and cook until golden brown on both sides.
4. Serve with sugar-free syrup, fresh berries, or topping of your choice.

Nutrition:

- **Calories:** 250
- **Total carbs:** 25 g
- **Net Carbs:** 23 g
- **Protein:** 25 g
- **Fat:** 4 g
- **Sugar:** 7 g
- **Fiber:** 2 g

13. Ham & Broccoli Breakfast Bake

Preparation Time: 10 minutes
Cooking Time: 35–40 minutes
Servings: 8
Ingredients:

- 8–10 eggs, beaten
- 4–6 cups small broccoli florets, blanch for 2 minutes, then drain well
- 1–2 cups ham, diced
- 1 cup mozzarella cheese, grated
- 1/3 cup green onion, sliced thin
- 1 tsp. all-purpose seasoning
- Fresh-ground black pepper, to taste
- Non-stick cooking spray

Directions:

1. Heat the oven to 375°F. Spray a 9x12-inch baking dish with cooking spray.
2. Put broccoli, ham, cheese, and onions into layers in the dish. Sprinkle with seasoning and pepper. Pour eggs over everything.
3. Using a fork, stir the mixture to make sure everything is coated with the egg.
4. Bake 35-40 minutes, or until eggs are set and the top is starting to brown. Serve immediately.

Nutrition:

- **Calories:** 159
- **Total Carbs:** 7 g
- **Net Carbs:** 5 g
- **Protein:** 15 g
- **Fat:** 9 g
- **Sugar:** 2 g
- **Fiber:** 2 g

14. Ham & Cheese Breakfast Biscuits

Preparation Time: 5 minutes
Cooking Time: 15 minutes
Servings: 4
Ingredients:

- 1 cup ham, diced
- 2 eggs
- ¾ cup mozzarella cheese, grated
- ½ cup low-fat cheddar cheese, grated
- ½ cup reduced-fat grated parmesan, grated

Directions:

1. Heat oven to 375°F. Line a baking sheet with parchment paper.
2. In a large bowl, combine the cheeses and eggs until fully combined. Stir in the ham.
3. Divide the mixture evenly into 8 parts and form it into round rolls. Bake 15–20 minutes or until cheese is completely melted and the rolls are nicely browned.

Nutrition:

- **Calories:** 192
- **Total Carbs:** 2 g
- **Protein:** 16 g
- **Fat:** 13 g
- **Sugar:** 0 g
- **Fiber:** 0 g

15. Italian Breakfast Bake

Preparation Time: 10 minutes
Cooking Time: 1 hour
Servings: 8
Ingredients:

- 19 oz. pkg. mild Italian sausages, remove casings
- 1 yellow onion, diced
- 8 eggs
- 2 cups half-and-half
- 2 cups reduced-fat cheddar cheese, grated
- ¼ cup fresh parsley, diced
- 2 tbsps. butter, divided
- 1/2 loaf bread, cut into cubes
- 1 tsp. salt
- ¼ tsp. pepper
- ¼ tsp. red pepper flakes
- Non-stick cooking spray

Directions:

1. Spray a 9x13-inch baking dish with cooking spray.
2. Melt 1 tbsp. butter in a skillet over medium heat. Add sausage and cook, breaking up with a spatula, until no longer pink. Transfer to a large bowl.
3. Add remaining tbsp. butter to the skillet with the onion and cook until soft, 3–5 minutes. Add to sausage with the cheese and bread cubes.
4. In a separate bowl, whisk together eggs, half-and-half, and seasonings. Pour over sausage mixture, tossing to mix all ingredients. Pour into the prepared baking dish, cover, and chill 2 hours or overnight.
5. Heat the oven to 350°F. Remove the cover and bake for 50–60 minutes or until a knife inserted in the center comes out clean. Serve immediately and garnished with parsley.

Nutrition:

- **Calories:** 300
- **Total Carbs:** 6 g
- **Net Carbs:** 5 g
- **Protein:** 22 g
- **Fat:** 20 g
- **Sugar:** 4 g
- **Fiber:** 1 g

CHAPTER 2:

Snacks, Sides, and Appetizers

1. Baked Banana Chips

Preparation Time: 10 minutes
Cooking Time: 2 hours
Servings: 2
Ingredients:

- 2 just-ripe bananas, sliced in 1/10-inch-thick rounds, or more as needed
- 1 tsp. lemon juice, or to taste

Directions:

1. Prepare the oven by heating it to 110°C or 225°F. Put parchment paper on a baking sheet.
2. Arrange banana slices on the prepared baking sheet. Make sure the slices don't touch each other. Brush lemon juices on slices.
3. Bake for 90 minutes in the oven. Check the bananas, lift the slices about one or two times to separate them from the paper. Keep baking for another 30–90 minutes until the bananas have dried out.
4. Allow the bananas to cool for at least 5 minutes until crispy.

Nutrition:

- **Calories:** 106
- **Cholesterol:** 0
- **Protein:** 1.3 g
- **Total fat:** 0.4 g
- **Sodium:** 1 mg
- **Total Carbohydrate:** 27.2 g

2. Baked Tortilla Chips

Preparation Time: 10 minutes
Cooking Time: 15 minutes
Servings: 6
Ingredients:

- 1 (12-ounce) package corn tortillas
- 1 tbsp. vegetable oil
- 3 tbsps. lime juice
- 1 tsp. ground cumin
- 1 tsp. chili powder
- 1 tsp. salt
- Salsas, for serving (optional)
- Guacamole, for serving (optional)

Directions:

1. Start preheating the oven to 175°C (350°F).
2. Slice each tortilla into 8 chip-sized wedges. On a cookie sheet, place the wedges in a single layer.
3. Mix well the lime juice and oil in a mister. Spray each tortilla wedge until slightly moist.
4. In a small bowl, mix the cumin, salt, and chili powder and dust on the chips.
5. Place in the oven to bake for about 7 minutes. Turn the pan and bake until the chips are crisp but not too brown, about 8 minutes longer. Best served with salsas, guacamole, or garnishes.

Nutrition:

- **Calories:** 147
- **Protein:** 3.3 g
- **Total fat:** 4.1 g
- **Sodium:** 418 mg
- **Total Carbohydrate:** 26 g
- **Cholesterol:** 0

3. Banana Oat Energy Bars

Preparation Time: 15 minutes
Cooking Time: 20 minutes
Servings: 12
Ingredients:

- 2 cups rolled oats
- 2 bananas, mashed
- 2 carrots, grated
- 1 apple, grated
- 1 cup unsweetened applesauce
- 1/2 cup chopped peanuts

Directions:

1. Preheat the oven to 175°C/350°F. Grease the 9x13-in. baking dish.
2. In a bowl, mix peanuts, applesauce, apple, carrots, bananas, and oats. Spread in prepped baking dish.
3. In the preheated oven, bake for 20 minutes till golden brown.

Nutrition:

- **Calories:** 124
- **Total fat:** 4 g
- **Sodium:** 10 mg
- **Total Carbohydrate:** 20 g
- **Cholesterol:** 0
- **Protein:** 3.6 g

4. Basil and Pesto Hummus

Preparation Time: 5 minutes
Cooking Time: 10 minutes
Servings: 5
Ingredients:

- 1 (16-ounce) garbanzo beans (chickpeas), drained and rinsed
- 1/2 cup basil leaves
- 1 garlic clove
- 1 tbsp. olive oil
- 1/2 tsp. balsamic vinegar
- 1/2 tsp. soy sauce
- Salt and ground black pepper to taste

Directions:

1. In a food processor, mix garlic, basil, and garbanzo beans, then pulse a few times. Scrape down the sides of the processor bowl using a spatula. Pulse again while drizzling in the olive oil. Stir in soy sauce and vinegar, and process until incorporated. Sprinkle pepper and salt to season.

Nutrition:

- **Calories:** 134
- **Total fat:** 3.8 g
- **Sodium:** 302 mg
- **Total Carbohydrate:** 2 g1
- **Cholesterol:** 0
- **Protein:** 4.7 g

5.   A New Green Bean Casserole

Preparation Time: 20 minutes
Cooking Time: 1 hour
Servings: 6
Ingredients:

- 1 1/2 pounds fresh green beans, trimmed
- 4 cups sliced onions
- 2 tbsps. balsamic vinegar, or more if needed
- 3 garlic cloves, chopped
- 2 tsps. white sugar
- 1 tsp. dried basil
- 1 tsp. dried oregano
- 1/4 cup shredded Parmesan cheese, or to taste
- ½ cup halved grape tomatoes

Directions:

1. Bring lightly salted water in a big pot to a boil, then cook green beans at a boil for 5–10 minutes, or until tender but still firm to the bite. Drain and turn to a 13"x9" dish.
2. In a skillet, cook and stir together oregano, basil, sugar, garlic, vinegar, and onions on medium heat for 5 minutes or until onions are translucent and tender. Lower heat to medium-low, then keep on cooking and stirring for 15–20 minutes longer, or until onions turn dark brown and very softened.
3. Set the oven to 200°C or 400°F.
4. Spread over green beans with onion mixture and put Parmesan cheese on top. Place tomatoes on top of the Parmesan cheese layer, with cut-side down.
5. In the preheated oven, bake for 35 minutes or until cheese has melted and bubbled.

Nutrition:

- **Calories:** 97
- **Cholesterol:** 2
- **Protein:** 4.6 g
- **Total fat:** 1.3 g
- **Sodium:** 70 mg
- **Total Carbohydrate:** 19.5 g

6. Cauliflower Fritters

Preparation Time: 10 minutes
Cooking Time: 14 minutes
Servings: 2
Ingredients:

- 5 cups chopped cauliflower florets
- 1/2 cup almond flour
- 1/2 tsp. baking powder
- ½ tsp. ground black pepper
- ½ tsp. salt
- 2 eggs, pastured

Directions:

1. Add chopped cauliflower in a blender or food processor, pulse until minced, and then tip the mixture into a bowl.
2. Add the remaining ingredients, stir well and then shape the mixture into 1/3-inch patties, an ice cream scoop of mixture per patty.
3. Switch on the air fryer, insert fryer basket, grease it with olive oil, then shut with its lid, set the fryer at 390°F, and preheat for 5 minutes.
4. Then open the fryer, add cauliflower patties in it in a single layer, spray oil over patties, close with its lid and cook for 14 minutes at 375°F until nicely golden and cooked, flipping the patties halfway through the frying.
5. Serve straight away with the dip.

Nutrition:

- **Calories:** 272
- **Carbs:** 57 g
- **Fat:** 0.3 g
- **Protein:** 11 g
- **Fiber:** 8 g

7.   Zucchini Fritters

Preparation Time: 20 minutes
Cooking Time: 12 minutes
Servings: 4
Ingredients:

- 2 medium zucchinis, ends trimmed
- 3 tbsps. almond flour
- 1 tbsp. salt
- 1 tsp. garlic powder
- ¼ tsp. paprika
- ¼ tsp. ground black pepper
- ¼ tsp. onion powder
- 1 egg, pastured
- Oil to grease

Directions:

1. Wash and pat dry the zucchini, then cut its ends and grate the zucchini.
2. Place grated zucchini in a colander, sprinkle with salt and let it rest for 10 minutes.
3. Then wrap zucchini in a kitchen cloth and squeeze moisture from it as much as possible and place dried zucchini in another bowl.
4. Add remaining ingredients into the zucchini and then stir until mixed.
5. Take fryer basket, line it with parchment paper, grease it with oil, and drop zucchini mixture on it by a spoonful, about 1-inch apart and then spray well with oil.
6. Switch on the air fryer, insert fryer basket, then shut with its lid, set the fryer at 360°F, and cook the fritter for 12 minutes until nicely golden and cooked, flipping the fritters halfway through the frying.
7. Serve straight away.

Nutrition:

- **Calories:** 57
- **Carbs:** 8 g
- **Fat:** 1 g
- **Protein:** 3 g
- **Fiber:** 1 g

8. Kale Chips

Preparation Time: 5 minutes
Cooking Time: 7 minutes
Servings: 2
Ingredients:

- 1 large bunch of kale
- ¾ tsp. red chili powder
- 1 tsp. salt
- ¾ tsp. ground black pepper
- Cooking spray

Directions:

1. Remove the hard spines from the kale leaves, then cut kale into small pieces and place them in a fryer basket.
2. Spray oil over kale, then sprinkle with salt, chili powder, and black pepper and toss until well mixed.
3. Switch on the air fryer, insert fryer basket, then shut with its lid, set the fryer at 375°F, and cook for 7 minutes until kale is crispy, shaking halfway through the frying.
4. When the air fryer beeps, open its lid, transfer kale chips onto a serving plate and serve.

Nutrition:

- **Calories:** 66.2
- **Carbs:** 7.3 g
- **Fat:** 4 g
- **Protein:** 2.5 g
- **Fiber:** 2.6 g

9.   Broccoli & Bacon Salad

Preparation Time: 10 minutes
Cooking Time: 0 minutes
Servings: 4
Ingredients:

- 2 cups broccoli, separated into florets
- 4 bacon slices, chopped and cooked crisp
- ½ cup cheddar cheese, cubed
- ¼ cup low-fat Greek yogurt
- 1/8 cup red onion, diced fine
- 1/8 cup almonds, sliced
- ¼ cup reduced-fat mayonnaise
- 1 tbsp. lemon juice
- 1 tbsp. apple cider vinegar
- 1 tbsp. granulated sugar substitute
- ¼ tsp. salt
- ¼ tsp. pepper

Directions:

1. In a large bowl, combine broccoli, onion, cheese, bacon, and almonds.
2. In a small bowl, whisk the remaining ingredients together until combined.
3. Pour dressing over broccoli mixture and stir. Cover and chill at least 1 hour before serving.

Nutrition:

- **Calories:** 217
- **Total Carbs:** 12 g
- **Net Carbs:** 10 g
- **Protein:** 11 g
- **Fat:** 14 g
- **Sugar:** 6 g
- **Fiber:** 2 g

10. Broccoli & Mushroom Salad

Preparation Time: 10 minutes
Cooking Time: 0 minutes
Servings: 4
Ingredients:

- 4 sun-dried tomatoes, cut in half
- 3 cups torn leaf lettuce
- 1 ½ cup broccoli florets
- 1 cup mushrooms, sliced
- 1/3 cup radishes, sliced
- 2 tbsps. water
- 1 tbsp. balsamic vinegar
- 1 tsp. vegetable oil
- ¼ tsp. chicken bouillon granules
- ¼ tsp. parsley
- ¼ tsp. dry mustard
- 1/8 tsp. cayenne pepper

Directions:

1. Place tomatoes in a small bowl and pour boiling water over, just enough to cover. Let stand 5 minutes, drain.
2. Chop tomatoes and place in a large bowl. Add lettuce, broccoli, mushrooms, and radishes.
3. In a jar with a tight-fitting lid, add the remaining ingredients and shake well. Pour over salad and toss to coat. Serve.

Nutrition:

- **Calories:** 54
- **Total Carbs:** 9 g
- **Net Carbs:** 7 g
- **Protein:** 3 g
- **Fat:** 2 g
- **Sugar:** 2 g
- **Fiber:** 2 g

11. Cantaloupe & Prosciutto Salad

Preparation Time: 15 minutes
Cooking Time: 0 minutes
Servings: 4
Ingredients:

- 6 mozzarella balls, quartered
- 1 medium cantaloupe, peeled and cut into small cubes
- 4 oz prosciutto, chopped
- 1 tbsp. fresh lime juice
- 1 tbsp. fresh mint, chopped
- 2 tbsps. extra virgin olive oil
- 1 tsp. honey
- Salt and pepper to taste

Directions:

1. In a large bowl, whisk together oil, lime juice, honey, and mint. Season with salt and pepper to taste.
2. Add the cantaloupe and mozzarella and toss to combine. Arrange the mixture on a serving plate and add prosciutto. Serve.

Nutrition:

- **Calories:** 240
- **Total Carbs:** 6 g
- **Protein:** 18 g
- **Fat:** 16 g
- **Sugar:** 4 g
- **Fiber:** 0 g

12. Radish Chips

Preparation Time: 5 minutes
Cooking Time: 20 minutes
Servings: 2
Ingredients:

- 8 oz. radish slices
- ½ tsp. garlic powder
- 1 tsp. salt
- ½ tsp. onion powder
- ½ tsp. ground black pepper
- Cooking spray

Directions:

1. Wash the radish slices, pat them dry, place them in a fryer basket, and then spray oil on them until well coated.
2. Sprinkle salt, garlic powder, onion powder, and black pepper over radish slices and then toss until well coated.
3. Switch on the air fryer, insert fryer basket, then shut with its lid, set the fryer at 370°F, and cook for 10 minutes, stirring the slices halfway through.
4. Then spray oil on radish slices, shake the basket and continue frying for 10 minutes, stirring the chips halfway through.
5. Serve straight away.

Nutrition:

- **Calories:** 21
- **Carbs:** 1 g
- **Fat:** 1.8 g
- **Protein:** 0.2 g
- **Fiber:** 0.4 g

13. Zucchini Fries

Preparation Time: 10 minutes
Cooking Time: 20 minutes
Servings: 4
Ingredients:

- 2 medium zucchinis
- ½ cup almond flour
- 1/8 tsp. ground black pepper
- ½ tsp. garlic powder
- 1/8 tsp. salt
- 1 tsp. Italian seasoning
- ½ cup grated parmesan cheese, reduced-fat
- 1 egg, pastured, beaten
- Oil to grease

Directions:

1. Switch on the air fryer, insert fryer basket, grease it with olive oil, then shut with its lid, set the fryer at 400°F, and preheat for 10 minutes.
2. Meanwhile, cut each zucchini in half and then cut each zucchini half into 4-inch-long pieces, each about ½-inch thick.
3. Place flour in a shallow dish, add the remaining ingredients except for the egg and stir until mixed.
4. Crack the egg in a bowl and then whisk until blended.
5. Working on one zucchini piece at a time, first dip it in the egg, then coat it in the almond flour mixture and place it on a wire rack.
6. Open the fryer, add zucchini pieces in it in a single layer, spray oil over zucchini, close with its lid and cook for 10 minutes until nicely golden and crispy, shaking halfway through the frying.
7. Cook the remaining zucchini pieces in the same manner and serve.

Nutrition:

- **Calories:** 147
- **Carbs:** 6 g
- **Fat:** 10 g
- **Protein:** 9 g
- **Fiber:** 2 g

14. Avocado Fries

Preparation Time: 10 minutes
Cooking Time: 20 minutes
Servings: 2
Ingredients:

- 1 medium avocado, pitted
- 1 egg
- 1/2 cup almond flour
- ¼ tsp. ground black pepper
- 1/2 tsp. salt
- 2 tsp. olive oil

Directions:

1. Switch on the air fryer, insert fryer basket, grease it with olive oil, then shut with its lid, set the fryer at 400°F, and preheat for 10 minutes.
2. Meanwhile, cut the avocado in half and then cut each half into wedges, each about ½-inch thick.
3. Place flour in a shallow dish, add salt and black pepper and stir until mixed.
4. Crack the egg in a bowl and then whisk until blended.
5. Working on one avocado piece at a time, first dip it in the egg, then coat it in the almond flour mixture and place it on a wire rack.
6. Open the fryer, add avocado pieces to it in a single layer, spray oil over avocado, close with its lid and cook for 10 minutes until nicely golden and crispy, shaking halfway through the frying.
7. When the air fryer beeps, open its lid, transfer avocado fries onto a serving plate and serve.

Nutrition:

- **Calories:** 251
- **Carbs:** 19 g
- **Fat:** 17 g
- **Protein:** 6 g
- **Fiber:** 7 g

15. Applesauce for the Freezer

Preparation Time: 15 minutes
Cooking Time: 25 minutes
Servings: 20
Ingredients:

- 3 1/2 pounds apples, peeled, cored, and quartered
- 1 cup water
- 1/4 cup dark brown sugar
- 1/4 cup white sugar, or less to taste
- 3 tbsps. lemon juice, or more to taste
- 1 (3-inch) piece cinnamon stick
- 4 lemon zest strips
- 1/2 tsp. salt

Directions:

1. Mix apples, lemon juice and zest, water, white sugar, brown sugar, cinnamon stick, and salt in a large pot. Put the lid on and let the mixture boil. Lower the heat to medium-low heat. Cook for 20–30 minutes until the fruit has softened.
2. Take off the heat. Discard the lemon strips and cinnamon stick. Crush apples with a potato masher.

Nutrition:

- **Calories:** 63
- **Total fat:** 0.1 g
- **Sodium:** 60 mg
- **Total Carbohydrate:** 16.6 g
- **Cholesterol:** 0 mg
- **Protein:** 0.2 g

16. Arizona Cactus and Beans

Preparation Time: 15 minutes
Cooking Time: 18 minutes
Servings: 6
Ingredients:

- 2 tsps. vegetable oil
- 2 potatoes, cut into small rectangles
- 1 cup shredded carrots
- 2 1/2 (15-oz.) jars nopalitos, drained
- 1 tbsp. chili powder
- 2 garlic cloves, minced
- 2 tsps. fenugreek seeds
- 2 tsps. ground coriander
- 1/2 tsp. ground cumin
- 1 (15-oz.) can pinto beans

Directions:

1. In a skillet, heat oil over moderate heat. Put in carrots and potatoes, then cook and stir for 10 minutes, until potatoes are softened.
2. Stir into the potato mixture with cumin, coriander, fenugreek seeds, garlic, chili powder, and nopalitos. Cook for 5 minutes while stirring often, until nopalitos are tender. Put in pinto beans and cook for 3 minutes while stirring gently until just heated through.

Nutrition:

- **Calories:** 160
- **Cholesterol:** 0 g
- **Protein:** 6.9 g
- **Total fat:** 2.7 g
- **Sodium:** 217 mg
- **Total Carbohydrate:** 30 g

17. Baked Potato

Preparation Time: 3 minutes
Cooking Time: 1 hour 30 minutes
Servings: 1
Ingredients:

- 1 baking potato

Directions:

1. Set the oven to 175°C or 350°F to preheat.
2. Scrub the potato and use a fork to prick it so that steam doesn't build up to make your potato explodes in the oven.
3. Bake for 1 1/2 hours.

Nutrition:

- **Calories:** 128
- **Protein:** 2.7 g
- **Sodium:** 7 mg
- **Total Carbohydrate:** 29.7 g
- **Cholesterol:** 0 mg
- **Total fat:** 0.1 g

18. Baked Sweet Potato Sticks

Preparation Time: 15minutes
Cooking Time: 40minutes
Servings: 8
Ingredients:
- 1 tbsp. olive oil
- 1/2 tsp. paprika
- 8 sweet potatoes, sliced lengthwise into quarters

Directions:
1. Heat the oven to 200°C (400°F). Grease a baking sheet lightly.
2. In a big bowl, combine paprika and olive oil. Put the potato sticks in and mix by hand to coat completely. Arrange on the prepared baking sheet.
3. Bake for 40 minutes in the oven.

Nutrition:
- **Calories:** 132
- **Total fat:** 1.9 g
- **Sodium:** 47 mg
- **Total Carbohydrate:** 27 g
- **Cholesterol:** 0 mg
- **Protein:** 2.6 g

CHAPTER 3:

Lunch

1. Peppered Broccoli Chicken

Preparation Time: 20 minutes
Cooking Time: 30 minutes
Servings: 4
Ingredients:

- 1 tbsp. sage (sliced)
- 1 cup broccoli florets
- 1 lb. (no bones and skin) chicken breast
- 3 garlic cloves
- 1 cup tomato passata
- Salt and black pepper to taste
- 2 tbsps. olive oil

Directions:

1. Put the instant pot on the "Sauté" option, then put the oil and cook it. After that, put the chicken and garlic then heats it for 5 minutes.
2. Put the other ingredients, then cover it and heat it for 25 minutes at a high temperature.
3. Release the pressure gradually for 10 minutes, then split them among your plates before eating.

Nutrition:

- **Calories:** 217
- **Fat:** 10.1 g
- **Fiber:** 1.8 g
- **Carbs:** 5.9 g
- **Protein:** 25.4 g

2.   Turkey Coriander Dish

Preparation Time: 20 minutes
Cooking Time: 20 minutes
Servings: 4
Ingredients:
- Half bunch coriander (sliced)
- 1 cup chard (sliced)
- 1 piece (no bones and skin) turkey breast
- 1 and a half cup coconut cream
- 2 pieces garlic cloves
- 1 tbsp. melted ghee

Directions:
1. Put the instant pot on the "Sauté" option, then put the ghee and cook it. After that, put the garlic and meat, then heat it for 5 minutes.
2. Put the other ingredients, then cover it and heat it for 25 minutes at a high temperature.
3. Release the pressure gradually for 10 minutes, then split them among your plates before eating.

Nutrition:
- **Calories:** 225
- **Fat:** 8.9 g
- **Fiber:** 0.2 g
- **Carbs:** 0.8 g
- **Protein:** 33.5 g

3. Flank Steak Beef

Preparation Time: 10 minutes
Cooking Time: 20 minutes
Servings: 4
Ingredients:

- 1 pound flank steaks, sliced
- ¼ cup xanthan gum
- 2 tsps. vegetable oil
- ½ tsp. ginger
- ½ cup soy sauce
- 1 tbsp. garlic, minced
- ½ cup water
- ¾ cup swerve, packed

Directions:

1. Preheat the Air fryer to 390°F and grease an Air fryer basket.
2. Coat the steaks with xanthan gum on both sides and transfer them into the Air fryer basket.
3. Cook for about 10 minutes and dish out on a platter.
4. Meanwhile, cook the rest of the ingredients for the sauce in a saucepan.
5. Bring to a boil and pour over the steak slices to serve.

Nutrition:

- **Calories:** 372
- **Fat:** 11.8 g
- **Carbs:** 1.8 g
- **Sugar:** 27.3 g
- **Protein:** 34 g
- **Sodium:** 871 mg

4. Sage Beef

Preparation Time: 10 minutes
Cooking Time: 30 minutes
Servings: 4
Ingredients:

- 2 lbs. beef stew meat, cubed
- 1 tbsp. sage, chopped
- 2 tbsps. butter, melted
- ½ tsp. coriander, ground
- ½ tbsp. garlic powder
- 1 tsp. Italian seasoning
- Salt and black pepper to the taste

Directions:

1. In the air fryer's pan, mix the beef with the sage, melted butter, and the other ingredients, introduce the pan in the fryer and cook at 360°F for 30 minutes.
2. Divide everything between plates and serve.

Nutrition:

- **Calories:** 290
- **Fat:** 11 g
- **Fiber:** 6 g
- **Carbs:** 20 g
- **Protein:** 29 g

5. Beef, Olives, and Tomatoes

Preparation Time: 10 minutes
Cooking Time: 35 minutes
Servings: 4
Ingredients:

- 2 lbs. beef stew meat, cubed
- 1 cup black olives, pitted and halved
- 1 cup cherry tomatoes, halved
- 1 tbsp. smoked paprika
- 3 tbsps. olive oil
- 1 tsp. coriander, ground
- Salt and black pepper to the taste

Directions:

1. In the air fryer's pan, mix the beef with the olives and the other ingredients, toss and cook at 390°F for 35 minutes.
2. Divide between plates and serve.

Nutrition:

- **Calories:** 291
- **Fat:** 12 g
- **Fiber:** 9 g
- **Carbs:** 20 g
- **Protein:** 26 g

6.   Easy Lime Lamb Cutlets

Preparation Time: 4 hours 20 minutes
Cooking Time: 8 minutes
Servings: 4
Ingredients:

- ¼ cup freshly squeezed lime juice
- 2 tbsps. lime zest
- 2 tbsps. chopped fresh parsley
- Sea salt and freshly ground black pepper, to taste
- 1 tbsp. extra virgin olive oil
- 12 lamb cutlets (about 1½ lbs./680 g in total)

Directions:

1. Combine the lime juice and zest, parsley, salt, black pepper, and olive oil in a large bowl. Stir to mix well.
2. Dunk the lamb cutlets in the bowl of the lime mixture, then toss to coat well. Wrap the bowl in plastic and refrigerate to marinate for at least 4 hours.
3. Preheat the oven to 450°F (235°C) or broil. Line a baking sheet with aluminum foil.
4. Remove the bowl from the refrigerator and let sit for 10 minutes, then discard the marinade. Arrange the lamb cutlets on the baking sheet.
5. Broil the lamb in the preheated oven for 8 minutes or until it reaches your desired doneness. Flip the cutlets with tongs to make sure they are cooked evenly.
6. Serve immediately.

Tip: If you are fancy about the spicy taste of the lamb cutlets, you can sprinkle the cooked cutlets with chipotle chili powder or red pepper flakes before serving.

Nutrition:

- **Calories:** 297
- **Fat:** 18.8 g
- **Protein:** 31.0 g
- **Carbs:** 1.0 g
- **Fiber:** 0 g
- **Sugar:** 0 g
- **Sodium:** 100 mg

7. Sumptuous Lamb and Pomegranate Salad

Preparation Time: 8 hours 35 minutes
Cooking Time: 30 minutes
Servings: 8
Ingredients:

- 1½ cups pomegranate juice
- 4 tbsps. olive oil, divided - 1 tbsp. ground cinnamon
- 1 tsp. cumin - 1 tbsp. ground ginger
- 3 garlic cloves, chopped
- Salt and freshly ground black pepper to taste
- 1 (4-pound/1.8-kg) lamb leg, deboned, butterflied, and fat trimmed
- 2 tbsps. pomegranate balsamic vinegar
- 2 tsps. Dijon mustard - ½ cup pomegranate seeds
- 5 cups baby kale
- 4 cups fresh green beans, blanched
- ¼ cup toasted walnut halves
- 2 fennel bulbs, thinly sliced
- 2 tbsps. Gorgonzola cheese

Directions:

1. Mix the pomegranate juice, 1 tbsp. of olive oil, cinnamon, cumin, ginger, garlic, salt, and black pepper in a large bowl. Stir to mix well.
2. Dunk the lamb leg in the mixture, press to coat well. Wrap the bowl in plastic and refrigerate to marinate for at least 8 hours.
3. Remove the bowl from the refrigerator and let it sit for 20 minutes. Pat the lamb dry with paper towels. Preheat the grill to high heat.
4. Brush the grill grates with 1 tbsp. of olive oil, then arrange the lamb on the grill grates. Grill for 30 minutes or until the internal temperature of the lamb reaches at least 145°F (63°C). Flip the lamb halfway through the cooking time.
5. Remove the lamb from the grill and wrap it with aluminum foil. Let stand for 15 minutes. Meanwhile, combine the vinegar, mustard, salt, black pepper, and remaining olive oil in a separate large bowl. Stir to mix well.
6. Add the remaining ingredients and lamb leg to the bowl and toss to combine well. Serve immediately.

Tips: You can use the same amount of sliced red grapes to replace the pomegranate seeds. If you don't have pomegranate balsamic vinegar, you can juice use the balsamic vinegar to replace it.
Nutrition:

- **Calories:** 380 **Fat:** 21.0 g **Protein:** 32.0 g **Carbs:** 16.0 g
- **Fiber:** 5.0 g **Sugar:** 6.0 g **Sodium:** 240 mg

8. Pork Spare Ribs

Preparation Time: 15 minutes
Cooking Time: 20 minutes
Servings: 6
Ingredients:

- 5–6 garlic cloves, minced
- ½ cup rice vinegar
- 2 tbsps. soy sauce
- Salt and ground black pepper, as required
- 12 1-inch pork spare ribs
- ½ cup cornstarch
- 2 tbsps. olive oil

Directions:

1. In a large bowl, mix together the garlic, vinegar, soy sauce, salt, and black pepper.
2. Add the ribs and generously coat with the mixture.
3. Refrigerate to marinate overnight.
4. In a shallow bowl, place the cornstarch.
5. Coat the ribs evenly with cornstarch and then drizzle with oil.
6. Set the temperature of the air fryer to 390°F. Grease an air fryer basket.
7. Arrange ribs into the prepared air fryer basket in a single layer.
8. Air fry for about 10 minutes per side.
9. Remove from air fryer and transfer the ribs onto serving plates.
10. Serve immediately.

Nutrition:

- **Calories:** 557
- **Carbohydrate:** 11 g
- **Protein:** 35 g
- **Fat:** 51.3 g
- **Sugar:** 0.1 g
- **Sodium:** 997 mg

9. Buttery Cod
Preparation Time: 13 minutes
Cooking Time: 0 minutes
Servings: 2
Ingredients:
- 2 (4-oz.) cod fillets
- ½ medium lemon, sliced
- 2 tbsps. salted butter; melted
- 1 tsp. Old Bay® seasoning

Directions:
1. Place cod fillets into a 6-inch round baking dish. Brush each fillet with butter and sprinkle with Old Bay® seasoning. Lay two lemon slices on each fillet.
2. Cover the dish with foil and place it into the air fryer basket. Adjust the temperature to 350°F and set the timer for 8 minutes.
3. Flip halfway through the cooking time. When cooked, the internal temperature should be at least 145°F. Serve warm.

Nutrition:
- **Calories:** 179
- **Protein:** 14 g
- **Fiber:** 0 g
- **Fat:** 11 g
- **Carbs:** 0 g

10. Lime Baked Salmon

Preparation Time: 22 minutes
Cooking Time: 0 minutes
Servings: 2
Ingredients:

- 2 (3-oz.) salmon fillets, skin removed
- ¼ cup sliced pickled jalapeños
- ½ medium lime, juiced
- 2 tbsps. chopped cilantro
- 1 tbsp. salted butter; melted
- ½ tsp. finely minced garlic
- 1 tsp. chili powder

Directions:

1. Place salmon fillets into a 6-inch round baking pan. Brush each with butter and sprinkle with chili powder and garlic.
2. Place jalapeño slices on top and around the salmon. Pour half of the lime juice over the salmon and cover with foil. Place pan into the air fryer basket. Adjust the temperature to 370°F and set the timer for 12 minutes.
3. When fully cooked, salmon should flake easily with a fork and reach an internal temperature of at least 145°F.
4. To serve, spritz with remaining lime juice and garnish with cilantro.

Nutrition:

- **Calories:** 167
- **Protein:** 18 g
- **Fiber:** 7 g
- **Fat:** 9 g
- **Carbs:** 6 g

11. Lime Trout and Shallots

Preparation Time: 17 minutes
Cooking Time: 0 minutes
Servings: 4
Ingredients:

- 4 trout fillets, boneless
- 3 garlic cloves, minced
- 6 shallots, chopped
- ½ cup butter, melted
- ½ cup olive oil
- 1 lime Juice
- A pinch of salt and black pepper

Directions:

1. In a pan that fits the air fryer, combine the fish with the shallots and the rest of the ingredients, toss gently.
2. Put the pan in the machine and cook at 390°F for 12 minutes, flipping the fish halfway.
3. Divide between plates and serve with a side salad.

Nutrition:

- **Calories:** 270
- **Fat:** 12 g
- **Fiber:** 4 g
- **Carbs:** 6 g
- **Protein:** 12 g

12. Fish and Salsa
Preparation Time: 20 minutes
Cooking Time: 0 minutes
Servings: 4
Ingredients:
- 4 sea bass fillets, boneless
- 3 garlic cloves, minced
- 3 tomatoes, roughly chopped
- 2 spring onions, chopped
- ¼ cup chicken stock
- 1 tbsp. balsamic vinegar
- 1 tbsp. olive oil
- A pinch of salt and black pepper

Directions:
1. In a blender, combine all the ingredients except the fish and pulse well.
2. Put the mix in a pan that fits the air fryer, add the fish, toss gently, introduce the pan in the fryer and cook at 380°F for 15 minutes. Divide between plates and serve.

Nutrition:
- **Calories:** 261
- **Fat:** 11 g
- **Fiber:** 4 g
- **Carbs:** 7 g
- **Protein:** 11 g

13. Crab Legs

Preparation Time: 20 minutes
Cooking Time: 0 minutes
Servings: 4
Ingredients:

- 3 lbs. crab legs
- ¼ cup salted butter; melted and divided
- ½ medium lemon juice
- ¼ tsp. garlic powder

Directions:

1. Take a large bowl, drizzle 2 tbsp. butter over crab legs. Place crab legs into the air fryer basket.
2. Adjust the temperature to 400°F and set the timer for 15 minutes. Shake the air fryer basket to toss the crab legs halfway through the cooking time.
3. In a small bowl, mix remaining butter, garlic powder, and lemon juice.
4. To serve, crack open crab legs and remove meat. Dip in lemon butter.

Nutrition:

- **Calories:** 123
- **Protein:** 17 g
- **Fiber:** 0 g
- **Fat:** 6 g
- **Carbs:** 4 g

14. Cajun Salmon

Preparation Time: 12 minutes
Cooking Time: 0 minutes
Servings: 2
Ingredients:

- 2 (4-oz.) salmon fillets, skin removed
- 2 tbsps. unsalted butter, melted
- 1 tsp. paprika
- ¼ tsp. ground black pepper
- ⅛ tsp. ground cayenne pepper
- ½ tsp. garlic powder

Directions:

1. Brush each fillet with butter. Combine remaining ingredients in a small bowl and then rub onto fish. Place fillets into the air fryer basket.
2. Adjust the temperature to 390°F and set the timer for 7 minutes. When fully cooked, the internal temperature will be 145°F. Serve immediately.

Nutrition:

- **Calories:** 253
- **Protein:** 29 g
- **Fiber:** 4 g
- **Fat:** 16 g
- **Carbs:** 4 g

15. Trout and Zucchinis

Preparation Time: 20 minutes
Cooking Time: 0 minutes
Servings: 4
Ingredients:

- 3 zucchinis, cut in medium chunks
- 4 trout fillets; boneless
- ¼ cup tomato sauce
- 1 garlic clove; minced
- ½ cup cilantro; chopped
- 1 tbsp. lemon juice
- 2 tbsps. olive oil
- Salt and black pepper to taste

Directions:

1. In a pan that fits your air fryer, mix the fish with the other ingredients, toss, introduce in the fryer and cook at 380°F for 15 minutes. Divide everything between plates and serve right away.

Nutrition:

- **Calories:** 220
- **Fat:** 12 g
- **Fiber:** 4 g
- **Carbs:** 6 g
- **Protein:** 9 g

16. BBQ Pork Ribs

Preparation Time: 15 minutes
Cooking Time: 26 minutes
Servings: 4
Ingredients:

- ¼ cup honey, divided
- ¾ cup BBQ sauce
- 2 tbsps. tomato ketchup
- 1 tbsp. Worcestershire sauce*
- 1 tbsp. soy sauce
- ½ tsp. garlic powder
- Freshly ground white pepper to taste
- 1¾ pounds pork ribs

Directions:

1. In a bowl, mix together 3 tbsps. of honey and the remaining ingredients except for pork ribs.
2. Add the pork ribs and generously coat with the mixture.
3. Refrigerate to marinate for about 20 minutes.
4. Set the temperature of the air fryer to 355°F. Grease an air fryer basket.
5. Arrange ribs into the prepared air fryer basket in a single layer.
6. Air fry for about 13 minutes per side.
7. Remove from air fryer and transfer the ribs onto plates.
8. Drizzle with the remaining honey and serve immediately.

Nutrition:

- **Calories:** 691
- **Carbohydrate:** 37.7 g
- **Protein:** 53.1 g
- **Fat:** 31.3 g
- **Sugar:** 32.2 g
- **Sodium:** 991 mg

Note - Worcestershire sauce* - The other ingredients that make up this savory sauce usually include onions, molasses, high fructose corn syrup (depending on the country of production), salt, garlic, tamarind, cloves, chili pepper extract, water, and natural flavorings.

17. Glazed Pork Shoulder

Preparation Time: 15 minutes
Cooking Time: 18 minutes
Servings: 5
Ingredients:

- 1/3 cup soy sauce
- 2 tbsps. sugar
- 1 tbsp. honey
- 2 pounds pork shoulder, cut into 1½-inch thick slices

Directions:

1. In a bowl, mix together all the soy sauce, sugar, and honey.
2. Add the pork and generously coat it with marinade.
3. Cover and refrigerate to marinate for about 4–6 hours.
4. Set the temperature of the air fryer to 335°F. Grease an air fryer basket.
5. Place the pork shoulder into the prepared air fryer basket.
6. Air fry for about 10 minutes and then another 6–8 minutes at 390°F.
7. Remove from the air fryer and transfer the pork shoulder onto a platter.
8. With a piece of foil, cover the pork for about 10 minutes before serving.
9. Enjoy.

Nutrition:

- **Calories:** 475
- **Carbohydrate:** 8 g
- **Protein:** 36.1 g
- **Fat:** 32.4 g
- **Sugar:** 7.1 g
- **Sodium:** 165 mg

18. Lamb Roast

Preparation Time: 10 minutes
Cooking Time: 8 hours
Servings: 6
Ingredients:

- 2 ¼ lbs. lamb leg
- 3 carrots, sliced
- 1 onion, chopped
- 2 garlic cloves, minced
- 2 rosemary sprigs
- ½ cup red wine
- 1 beef stock cube
- Salt and pepper to taste

Directions:

1. Season the lamb generously with salt and pepper.
2. Add the lamb to your Slow Cooker.
3. Place the remaining ingredients in a bowl, crumble the stock cube inside, stir to combine, and pour over the lamb.
4. Add the rosemary sprigs inside and put the lid on.
5. Cook for 8 hours on LOW.
6. Open the lid and shred the lamb inside the pot. Stir to make sure it is equally moist.
7. Serve and enjoy.

Nutrition:

- **Calories:** 270
- **Total fat:** 7 g
- **Carbs:** 11 g
- **Protein:** 34 g
- **Fiber:** 2 g

19. Beef and Chorizo Burger

Preparation Time: 25 minutes
Cooking Time: 0 minutes
Servings: 4
Ingredients:

- 5 pickled jalapeños slices; chopped
- ¼ lb. Mexican-style ground chorizo
- ¾lb. 80/20 ground beef
- ¼ cup chopped onion
- ¼ tsp. cumin
- 1 tsp. minced garlic
- 2 tsps. chili powder

Directions:

1. Take a large bowl, mix all ingredients. Divide the mixture into four sections and form them into burger patties.
2. Place burger patties into the air fryer basket, working in batches if necessary. Adjust the temperature to 375°F and set the timer for 15 minutes.
3. Flip the patties halfway through the cooking time. Serve warm.

Nutrition:

- **Calories:** 291
- **Protein:** 26 g
- **Fiber:** 9 g
- **Fat:** 13 g
- **Carbs:** 7 g

20. Peppered Chicken Breast with Basil

Preparation Time: 10 minutes
Cooking Time: 20 minutes
Servings: 4
Ingredients:

- ¼ cup red bell peppers
- 1 cup chicken stock
- 2 pieces (no skin and bones) chicken breasts
- 4 pieces garlic cloves (crushed)
- 1 and a half tbsp. basil (crushed)
- 1 tbsp. chili powder

Directions:

1. In the instant pot, combine the all ingredients, then cover them and cook for 25 minutes at a high temperature.
2. Release the pressure quickly for 5 minutes, then split them among your plates before eating.

Nutrition:

- **Calories:** 230
- **Fat:** 12.4 g
- **Fiber:** 0.8 g
- **Carbs:** 2.7 g
- **Protein:** 33.2 g

21. Homemade Hamburgers

Preparation Time: 30–35 minutes
Cooking Time: 60 minutes
Servings: 6
Ingredients:

- ¼ cup barbecue sauce
- ¼ cup chopped onion
- ¼ cup ketchup
- ¼ tsp. pepper
- ½ cup fat-free milk
- ½ cup water
- 1 cup dry bread crumbs
- 1 lb. 90% lean ground beef
- 1 tbsp. vinegar
- 1 tbsp. Worcestershire sauce
- 3 tbsp. brown sugar

Directions:

1. In a good-sized mixing bowl, moisten bread crumbs with milk.
2. Put in ground beef, onion, and pepper. Combine thoroughly. Set aside.
3. In a mixing bowl, make the sauce by mixing together completely brown sugar, vinegar, ketchup, Worcestershire sauce, barbecue sauce, and water.
4. Mould hamburger mixture into 6 patties.
5. Lay in a single layer in the baking dish.
6. Drizzle barbecue sauce over patties.
7. Cover and bake at 375°F for approximately half an hour.
8. Take out the cover and bake another approximately half an hour, basting intermittently with sauce.

Nutrition:

- **Calories:** 255
- **Total fat:** 7 g
- **Cholesterol:** 45 mg
- **Sodium:** 445 mg
- **Potassium:** 395 g
- **Total Carbs:** 28 g
- **Dietary Fiber:** 1 g
- **Sugar:** 14 g
- **Protein:** 18 g
- **Phosphorus:** 190 g

22. Lasagna

Preparation Time: approximately half an hour
Cooking Time: 3 hours
Servings: 8
Ingredients:

- ½ cup shredded Parmesan cheese
- 1 moderate onion, chopped
- 1 cup skim cottage cheese
- 1 lb. lean ground beef
- 1 tsp. garlic powder
- 1 tsp. onion powder
- 1½ cups shredded mozzarella cheese, divided
- 15-oz. can tomato sauce
- 2 tsps. Italian seasoning
- 28-oz. can crushed tomatoes
- 6–8 lasagna noodles, uncooked, divided
- Salt and pepper to taste
- Cooking spray

Directions:

1. Cover crock thoroughly with non-stick spray.
2. Saute ground beef with onion. Season with salt and pepper.
3. Put in the crushed tomatoes, tomato sauce, Italian seasoning, garlic powder, and onion powder to the browned beef/onion mixture and simmer on low for approximately 5 minutes.
4. While the sauce is simmering, combine the 1 cup cottage cheese and 1 cup of the shredded mozzarella cheese. Save for later.
5. In the bottom of your crock, add ⅓ of the sauce.
6. Cover the bottom of the crock with noodles.
7. Spread half of the cottage cheese/mozzarella mixture over the noodles and add ⅓ of the sauce again.
8. Put in another layer of noodles, cottage cheese/mozzarella mixture, and residual sauce.
9. Cook on low for approximately 3 hours.
10. Approximately 20 minutes before serving, sprinkle the top with residual ½ cup mozzarella cheese and the Parmesan cheese.

Nutrition:

- **Calories:** 306 **Total fat:** 10 g **Cholesterol:** 51 mg **Sodium:** 936 mg
- **Potassium:** 397 g **Total Carbs:** 29 **Dietary Fiber:** 3.7 g **Sugar:** 7 g
- **Protein:** 24 g **Phosphorus:** 260 g

23. Meat Pasties

Preparation Time: approximately half an hour
Cooking Time: 60 minutes
Servings: 12
Ingredients:
Dough:
- ½ cup trans-fat-free shortening
- ½ tsp. salt
- 2 cups all-purpose flour
- 7 tbsps. fat-free milk, or more

Filling:
- ¾ lb. 90% lean ground beef
- 1 tbsp. chopped bell pepper
- 1 tbsp. chopped celery
- 1 tsp. dried basil
- 1 tsp. dried oregano
- 2 tbsps. barbecue sauce, lowest sodium available
- 2 tbsps. chopped onion

Directions:
1. Mix all ingredients for the dough and mix thoroughly. Put in as much milk as needed to make a soft dough.
2. Separate the dough into four parts. Roll each part out thin and cut into three 6-inch circles for a total of 12.
3. Mix all filling ingredients in a frying pan and cook until meat has browned.
4. Place 1 tbsp. meat in each circle. Moisten edges of dough with water and fold in half to make a turnover. Seal edges with a fork. Prick top to allow steam to escape. Place on a non-oil-coated cookie sheet.
5. Bake at 375°F for 40 minutes. Serve hot or cold.

Nutrition:
- **Calories:** 135
- **Total fat:** 3 g
- **Cholesterol:** 15 mg
- **Sodium:** 140 mg
- **Potassium:** 145 g
- **Total Carbs:** 18 g
- **Dietary Fiber:** 1 g
- **Sugar:** 2 g
- **Protein:** 8 g
- **Phosphorus:** 80 g

CHAPTER 4:

Dinner

1. Coconut Chicken

Preparation Time: 10 minutes
Cooking Time: 4 hours
Servings: 6
Ingredients:

- 2 garlic cloves, minced
- Fresh cilantro, minced (as desired, for garnish)
- 1/2 cup light coconut milk
- 6 tbsps. sweetened coconut, shredded and toasted
- 2 tbsps. brown sugar
- 6 (about 1–1/2 pounds) boneless, skinless chicken thighs
- 2 tbsps. reduced-sodium soy sauce
- 1/8 tsp. ground cloves

Directions:

1. Mix brown sugar, 1/2 cup light coconut milk, 2 tbsps. soy sauce, 1/8 tsp. ground cloves and 2 minced garlic cloves in a bowl.
2. Add 6 boneless chicken thighs into a Crockpot.
3. Now pour the mixture of coconut milk over chicken thighs. Cover the cooker and cook for about 4–5 hours on low.
4. Serve coconut chicken with cilantro and coconut; enjoy!

Nutrition:

- **Calories:** 201
- **Fat:** 10 g
- **Total carbs:** 6 g
- **Protein:** 21 g

2.   Spicy Lime Chicken

Preparation Time: 10 minutes
Cooking Time: 3 hours
Servings: 6
Ingredients:

- 3 tbsps. lime juice
- Fresh cilantro leaves (as desired, for garnish)
- 1–1/2 pounds (about 4) boneless, skinless chicken breast halves
- 1 tsp. lime zest, grated
- 2 cups chicken broth
- 1 tbsp. chili powder

Directions:

1. Add chicken breast halves into a slow cooker.
2. Add 1 tbsp. chili powder, 3 tbsps. lime juice and 2 cups chicken broth in a small bowl; mix well and pour over chicken.
3. Cover the cooker and cook for about 3 hours on low. Once done, take the chicken out from the cooker and let it cool.
4. Once cooled, shred chicken by using forks and transfer back to the Crockpot.
5. Stir in 1 tsp. grated lime zest. Serve spicy lime chicken with cilantro, and enjoy!

Nutrition:

- **Calories:** 132
- **Fat:** 3 g
- **Total carbs:** 2 g
- **Protein:** 23 g

3.   Lemon Chicken with Basil

Preparation Time: 10 minutes
Cooking Time: 1 hour
Servings: 4
Ingredients:

- 1 kg chopped chicken
- 2 lemons
- 2 cups basil
- Salt and ground pepper
- 1 tbsp. extra virgin olive oil

Direction:

1. Put the chicken in a bowl with a jet of extra virgin olive oil.
2. Put salt, pepper, and basil.
3. Bind well and let stand for at least 30 minutes, stirring occasionally.
4. Put the pieces of chicken in the air fryer basket and take the air fryer.
5. Select 30 minutes.
6. Move occasionally.
7. Take out and put another batch.
8. Repeat the same process.

Nutrition:

- **Calories:** 1,440
- **Fat:** 74.9 g
- **Carbs:** 122.0 g
- **Protein:** 68.6 g

4. Chicken Thighs

Preparation Time: 10 minutes
Cooking Time: 20 minutes
Servings: 2
Ingredients:

- 4 chicken thighs
- Salt
- Pepper
- 1 tbsp. mustard
- ¼ tsp. paprika

Direction:

1. Before using the pot, it is convenient to turn it on for 5 minutes to heat it. Marinate the thighs with salt, pepper, mustard, and paprika. Put your thighs in the air fryer for 10 minutes at 380°F.
2. After the time, turn the thighs and fry for 10 more minutes. If necessary, you can use an additional 5 minutes depending on the size of the thighs so that they are well cooked.

Nutrition:

- **Calories:** 72
- **Fat:** 2.36 g
- **Carbs:** 0 g
- **Protein:** 11.78 g

5. Barbecue Pork Loin

Preparation Time: 10 minutes, plus 20 minutes marinating time
Cooking Time: 35 minutes
Servings: 6
Ingredients:

- 1½ pounds boneless pork sirloin roast
- 1 cup white vinegar
- 3 small garlic cloves, pressed
- 1 tbsp. creole seasoning
- ½ tsp. smoked paprika
- ½ tsp. cayenne pepper
- ½ cup chicken broth (here) or store-bought low-sodium chicken broth, plus more as needed
- ½ cup Barbecue Sauce, plus more for serving

Directions:

1. Preheat the oven to 400°F.
2. In a medium bowl, combine the pork, vinegar, and garlic. Set aside to marinate for 10 minutes.
3. Remove the pork from the marinade, shaking off any remaining vinegar, and transfer to a rimmed baking sheet.
4. Massage the pork all over with the Creole seasoning, paprika, and cayenne. Cover and set aside for 20 minutes.
5. In a Dutch oven, bring the broth to a simmer over high heat.
6. Add the pork and cook for 2 to 3 minutes per side, or until lightly browned. If the broth runs low, to keep the pork moist, add ¼ cup when turning.
7. Cover the pot, transfer to the oven, and cook for 30 minutes or until the pork is opaque.
8. Cover with the barbecue sauce, return to the oven, and cook for 5 to 7 minutes, or until a nice crust forms on the exterior.
9. Transfer the pork to a cutting board. Let rest for 5 to 10 minutes.
10. Slice the pork and serve with extra barbecue sauce.

Nutrition:

- **Calories:** 204
- **Total fat:** 7 g
- **Cholesterol:** 75 mg
- **Sodium:** 134 mg
- **Total Carbs:** 9 g
- **Sugar:** 6 g **Fiber:** 0 g
- **Protein:** 23 g

6. Pulled Pork Loin

Preparation Time: 30 minutes
Cooking Time: 35 minutes
Servings: 8
Ingredients:

- 2 pounds boneless pork sirloin roast
- 1 tbsp. ground mustard seeds
- ½ cup chicken broth (here) or store-bought low-sodium chicken broth
- 1 medium zucchini, grated
- 1 medium carrot, grated
- 1 medium onion, chopped
- 2 medium tomatoes, chopped
- ½ cup tomato paste
- ½ cup apple cider vinegar
- 2 tbsps. pepper sauce
- 1 tbsp. Worcestershire sauce
- 2 garlic cloves, minced
- 1 tsp. old bay seasoning
- Savory Skillet Corn Bread (optional, for serving)
- Spicy Mustard Greens (optional, for serving)

Directions:

1. Massage the pork all over with the mustard seeds and set aside for 20 minutes.
2. Select the "Sauté" setting on an electric pressure cooker, and combine the chicken broth, zucchini, carrot, onion, tomatoes, tomato paste, vinegar, pepper sauce, Worcestershire sauce, garlic, and seasoning. Cook, stirring often, for 5 minutes, or until the vegetables are softened.
3. Add the pork, close and lock the lid, and set the pressure valve to sealing.
4. Change to the Manual/Pressure Cook setting, and cook for 30 minutes.
5. Once cooking is complete, quick-release the pressure. Carefully remove the lid.
6. Transfer the pork to a clean, flat surface, and shred the meat using two forks.
7. Return the pork to the pressure cooker and mix it into the juices.
8. Serve with Savory Skillet Corn Bread and Spicy Mustard Greens.

Nutrition:

- **Calories:** 282 **Total fat:** 19 g
- **Cholesterol:** 70 mg **Sodium:** 127 mg
- **Total Carbs:** 8 g
- **Sugar:** 5 g
- **Fiber:** 2 g
- **Protein:** 21 g

7.   Creole Braised Sirloin

Preparation Time: 15 minutes
Cooking Time: 40 minutes
Servings: 4
Ingredients:

- 1 pound beef round sirloin tip, cut into 4 strips
- ¼ tsp. freshly ground black pepper
- 2 cups chicken broth (here) or store-bought low-sodium chicken broth, divided
- 1 medium onion, chopped
- 1 celery stalk, coarsely chopped
- 1 medium green bell pepper, coarsely chopped
- 2 garlic cloves, minced
- 4 medium tomatoes, coarsely chopped
- 1 bunch mustard greens including stems, coarsely chopped
- 1 tbsp. creole seasoning
- ¼ tsp. red pepper flakes
- 2 bay leaves

Directions:

1. Preheat the oven to 450°F.
2. Massage the beef all over with black pepper.
3. In a Dutch oven, bring 1 cup of broth to a simmer over medium heat.
4. Add the onion, celery, bell pepper, and garlic and cook, stirring often, for 5 minutes, or until the vegetables are softened.
5. Add the tomatoes, mustard greens, Creole seasoning, and red pepper flakes and cook for 3 to 5 minutes, or until the greens are wilted.
6. Add the bay leaves, beef, and remaining 1 cup of broth.
7. Cover the pot, transfer to the oven, and cook for 30 minutes or until the juices run clear when you pierce the beef.
8. Remove the beef from the oven and let rest for 5 to 7 minutes. Discard the bay leaves.
9. Thinly slice the beef and serve.

Nutrition:

- **Calories:** 202
- **Total fat:** 5 g
- **Cholesterol:** 60 mg
- **Sodium:** 129 mg
- **Total Carbs:** 14 g
- **Sugar:** 7 g
- **Fiber:** 5 g
- **Protein:** 28 g

8.   Crispy Chicken Wings

Preparation Time: 10 minutes
Cooking Time: 20 minutes
Servings: 4
Ingredients:

- 1 tbsp. gluten-free baking powder
- 3/4 tsp. sea salt
- 2 lbs. chicken wings
- 1/4 tsp. black pepper

Directions:

1. Preheat the Air Fryer to 370°F. Merge the chicken wings, baking powder, sea salt, and black pepper.
2. Pour some grease on the Air Fryer basket. Arrange the wings in batches into the Air Fryer basket and cook at 250°F for 15 minutes.
3. Shake the Air Fryer or turn the wings to the other side and cook for another 15 minutes for the wings to be well cooked.
4. Serve.

Nutrition:

- **Calories:** 275
- **Carbs:** 9 g
- **Fat:** 17 g
- **Protein:** 13 g

9. Herb Butter Lamb Chops

Preparation Time: 10 minutes
Cooking Time: 5 minutes
Servings: 4
Ingredients:

- 4 lamb chops
- 1 tsp. rosemary, chopped
- 1 tbsp. butter
- Pepper
- Salt

Directions:

1. Season lamb chops with pepper and salt.
2. Place the dehydrating tray in a multi-level air fryer basket and place the basket in the instant pot.
3. Place lamb chops on dehydrating tray.
4. Seal pot with air fryer lid and select air fry mode, then set the temperature to 400°F and timer for 5 minutes.
5. Mix together butter and rosemary and spread overcooked lamb chops.
6. Serve and enjoy.

Nutrition:

- **Calories:** 278
- **Fat:** 12.8 g
- **Carbohydrates:** 0.2 g
- **Sugar:** 0 g
- **Protein:** 38 g
- **Cholesterol:** 129 mg

10. Tuna Zoodle Casserole

Preparation Time: 30 minutes
Cooking Time: 0 minutes
Servings: 4
Ingredients:

- 1 oz. pork rinds, finely ground
- 2 medium zucchini, spiralized
- 2 (5-oz.) cans albacore tuna
- ¼ cup diced white onion
- ¼ cup chopped white mushrooms
- 2 stalks celery, finely chopped
- ½ cup heavy cream
- ½ cup vegetable broth
- 2 tbsps. full-fat mayonnaise
- 2 tbsps. salted butter
- ½ tsp. red pepper flakes
- ¼ tsp. xanthan gum

Directions:

1. In a large saucepan over medium heat, melt butter. Add onion, mushrooms, and celery and sauté until fragrant, about 3–5 minutes.
2. Pour in heavy cream, vegetable broth, mayonnaise, and xanthan gum. Reduce heat and continue cooking an additional 3 minutes until the mixture begins to thicken.
3. Add red pepper flakes, zucchini, and tuna. Turn off heat and stir until zucchini noodles are coated.
4. Pour into a 4-cup round baking dish. Top with ground pork rinds and cover the top of the dish with foil. Place into the air fryer basket. Adjust the temperature to 370°F and set the timer for 15 minutes.
5. When 3 minutes remain, remove the foil to brown the top of the casserole. Serve warm.

Nutrition:

- **Calories:** 339
- **Protein:** 17 g
- **Fiber:** 8 g
- **Fat:** 21 g
- **Carbs:** 1 g

11. Sea Bass and Rice

Preparation Time: 10 minutes
Cooking Time: 20 minutes
Servings: 4
Ingredients:

- 1 lb. sea bass fillets, boneless, skinless, and cubed
- 1 cup wild rice
- 2 cups chicken stock
- 2 scallions, chopped
- 1 red bell pepper, chopped
- 1 tsp. turmeric powder
- 1 tbsp. chives, chopped
- Salt and black pepper to the taste
- A drizzle of olive oil

Directions:

1. Grease the air fryer's pan with the oil, add the fish, rice, stock, and the other ingredients, toss gently, and cook at 380°F and cook for 20 minutes, stirring halfway.
2. Divide between plates and serve.

Nutrition:

- **Calories:** 290
- **Fat:** 12 g
- **Fiber:** 2 g
- **Carbs:** 16 g
- **Protein:** 19 g

12. Sea Bass and Cauliflower

Preparation Time: 5 minutes
Cooking Time: 20 minutes
Servings: 4
Ingredients:

- 1 lb. sea bass fillets, boneless and cubed
- 1 cup cauliflower florets
- 2 tbsps. butter, melted
- 1 tsp. garam masala
- ½ cup chicken stock
- 1 tbsp. parsley, chopped
- Salt and black pepper to the taste

Directions:

1. In your air fryer, combine the fish with the cauliflower and the other ingredients, toss gently, and cook at 380°F for 20 minutes.
2. Divide everything between plates and serve.

Nutrition:

- **Calories:** 272
- **Fat:** 4 g
- **Fiber:** 3 g
- **Carbs:** 14 g
- **Protein:** 4 g

13. Shrimp, Tomatoes, and Sprouts

Preparation Time: 5 minutes
Cooking Time: 10 minutes
Servings: 4
Ingredients:

- 1 lb. shrimp, peeled and deveined
- 1 cup cherry tomatoes, halved
- 1 cup Brussels sprouts, trimmed and halved
- 2 tbsps. butter, melted
- 1 tsp. red pepper flakes, crushed
- 1 tsp. coriander, ground
- Salt and black pepper to the taste
- ½ tsp. Italian seasoning
- 1 tbsp. cilantro, chopped

Directions:

1. In your air fryer, combine the shrimp with the tomatoes, sprouts, and the other ingredients, toss gently, and cook at 380°F for 10 minutes.
2. Divide everything into bowls and serve.

Nutrition:

- **Calories:** 219
- **Fat:** 6 g
- **Fiber:** 4 g
- **Carbs:** 14 g
- **Protein:** 15 g

14. Tabasco Shrimp

Preparation Time: 5 minutes
Cooking Time: 10 minutes
Servings: 4
Ingredients:

- 1 lb. big shrimp, peeled and deveined
- 1 tsp. cayenne pepper
- 2 tbsps. butter, melted
- 1 tsp. Tabasco sauce
- Salt and black pepper to the taste
- 1 tbsp. parsley, chopped

Directions:

1. In your air fryer, combine the shrimp with the cayenne, butter, and the other ingredients, toss and cook at 370°F for 10 minutes.
2. Divide into bowls and serve right away.

Nutrition:

- **Calories:** 210
- **Fat:** 7 g
- **Fiber:** 6 g
- **Carbs:** 13 g
- **Protein:** 8 g

15. Tilapia and Sauce

Preparation Time: 5 minutes
Cooking Time: 15 minutes
Servings: 4
Ingredients:
- 1 lb. tilapia fillets, boneless and cubed
- 1 cup tomato passata
- 1 tbsp. oregano, chopped
- 4 garlic cloves, minced
- Salt and black pepper to the taste
- 2 tbsps. butter, melted

Directions:
1. In your air fryer's pan, combine the tilapia with the tomato passata and the other ingredients, toss and cook at 380°F for 15 minutes.
2. Divide everything between plates and serve.

Nutrition:
- **Calories:** 210
- **Fat:** 11 g
- **Fiber:** 12 g
- **Carbs:** 16 g
- **Protein:** 9 g

16. Cabbage Wedges

Preparation Time: 10 minutes
Cooking Time: 29 minutes
Servings: 6
Ingredients:

- 1 small head of green cabbage
- 6 bacon strips, thick-cut, pastured
- 1 tsp. onion powder
- ½ tsp. ground black pepper
- 1 tsp. garlic powder
- ¾ tsp. salt
- 1/4 tsp. red chili flakes
- 1/2 tsp. fennel seeds
- 3 tbsps. olive oil

Directions:

1. Switch on the air fryer, insert fryer basket, grease it with olive oil, then shut with its lid, set the fryer at 350°F, and preheat for 5 minutes.
2. Open the fryer, add bacon strips in it, close with its lid and cook for 10 minutes until nicely golden and crispy, turning the bacon halfway through the frying.
3. Meanwhile, prepare the cabbage and for this, remove the outer leaves of the cabbage and then cut it into eight wedges, keeping the core intact.
4. Prepare the spice mix and for this, place onion powder in a bowl, add black pepper, garlic powder, salt, red chili, and fennel and stir until mixed.
5. Drizzle cabbage wedges with oil and then sprinkle with spice mix until well coated.
6. When the air fryer beeps, open its lid, transfer bacon strips to a cutting board and let it rest.
7. Add seasoned cabbage wedges into the fryer basket, close with its lid, then cook for 8 minutes at 400°F, flip the cabbage, spray with oil and continue air frying for 6 minutes until nicely golden and cooked.
8. When done, transfer cabbage wedges to a plate.
9. Chop the bacon, sprinkle it over cabbage and serve.

Nutrition:

- **Calories:** 123
- **Carbs:** 2 g
- **Fat:** 11 g
- **Protein:** 4 g
- **Fiber:** 0 g

17. Rosemary Lemon Lamb Chops

Preparation Time: 10 minutes
Cooking Time: 6 minutes
Servings: 2
Ingredients:

- 2 lamb chops
- 1 tbsp. dried rosemary
- 2 tbsps. lemon juice

Directions:

1. Mix together rosemary and lemon juice and brush over lamb chops.
2. Place the dehydrating tray in a multi-level air fryer basket and place the basket in the instant pot.
3. Place lamb chops on dehydrating tray.
4. Seal pot with air fryer lid and select air fry mode, then set the temperature to 400°F and timer for 6 minutes. Turn lamb chops halfway through.
5. Serve and enjoy.

Nutrition:

- **Calories:** 260
- **Fat:** 10.3 g
- **Carbohydrates:** 1.4 g
- **Sugar:** 0.3 g
- **Protein:** 38.1 g
- **Cholesterol:** 122 mg

18. Herb Garlic Lamb Chops

Preparation Time: 10 minutes
Cooking Time: 6 minutes
Servings: 3
Ingredients:

- 3 lamb loin chops
- 1 tbsp. lemon juice
- 1 tbsp. lemon zest, grated
- 2 tsps. dried rosemary
- 1 tsp. dried thyme
- 1 tbsp. olive oil
- 2 tsps. garlic, minced

Directions:

1. Mix together lemon juice, lemon zest, rosemary, thyme, oil, and garlic, and rub over lamb chops.
2. Place the dehydrating tray in a multi-level air fryer basket and place the basket in the instant pot.
3. Place lamb chops on dehydrating tray.
4. Seal pot with air fryer lid and select air fry mode, then set the temperature to 400°F and timer for 6 minutes. Turn lamb chops halfway through.
5. Serve and enjoy.

Nutrition:

- **Calories:** 300
- **Fat:** 14.8 g
- **Carbohydrates:** 1.9 g
- **Sugar:** 0.3 g
- **Protein:** 38.2 g
- **Cholesterol:** 122 mg

19. Delicious Lamb Chops

Preparation Time: 10 minutes
Cooking Time: 8 minutes
Servings: 4
Ingredients:

- 1 lb. lamb chops
- 2 tbsps. lemon juice
- 2 tbsps. olive oil
- 1 tsp. ground coriander
- 1 tsp. oregano
- 1 tsp. thyme
- 1 tsp. rosemary
- 1 tsp. salt

Directions:

1. Add lamb chops and remaining ingredients into the zip-lock bag. Shake well and place it in the refrigerator for 1 hour.
2. Place the dehydrating tray in a multi-level air fryer basket and place the basket in the instant pot.
3. Place lamb chops on dehydrating tray.
4. Seal pot with air fryer lid and select air fry mode, then set the temperature to 400°F and timer for 8 minutes. Turn lamb chops halfway through.
5. Serve and enjoy.

Nutrition:

- **Calories:** 276
- **Fat:** 15.5 g
- **Carbohydrates:** 0.8 g
- **Sugar:** 0.2 g
- **Protein:** 32 g
- **Cholesterol:** 102 mg

20. Pork Tenderloin with Bell Peppers

Preparation Time: 20 minutes
Cooking Time: 15 minutes
Servings: 3
Ingredients:

- 1 large red bell pepper, seeded and cut into thin strips
- 1 red onion, thinly sliced
- 2 tsps. Herbs de Provence
- Salt and ground black pepper, as required
- 1 tbsp. olive oil
- 10 ½-oz pork tenderloin, cut into 4 pieces
- ½ tbsp. Dijon mustard

Directions:

1. In a bowl, add the bell pepper, onion, Herbs de Provence, salt, black pepper, and ½ tbsp. of oil and toss to coat well.
2. Rub the pork pieces with mustard, salt, and black pepper.
3. Drizzle with the remaining oil.
4. Set the temperature of the air fryer to 390°F. Grease an air fryer pan.
5. Place bell pepper mixture into the prepared Air Fryer pan and top with the pork pieces.
6. Air fry for about 15 minutes, flipping once halfway through.
7. Remove from air fryer and transfer the pork mixture onto serving plates.
8. Serve hot.

Nutrition:

- **Calories:** 218
- **Carbohydrate:** 7.1 g
- **Protein:** 27.7 g
- **Fat:** 8.8 g
- **Sugar:** 3.7 g
- **Sodium:** 110 mg

21. Pork Tenderloin with Bacon & Veggies

Preparation Time: 20 minutes
Cooking Time: 28 minutes
Servings: 3
Ingredients:

- 3 potatoes
- ¾ pound frozen green beans
- 6 bacon slices
- 3 6-ounces pork tenderloins
- 2 tbsps. olive oil

Directions:

1. Set the temperature of the air fryer to 390°F. Grease an air fryer basket.
2. With a fork, pierce the potatoes.
3. Place potatoes into the prepared air fryer basket and air fry for about 15 minutes.
4. Wrap one bacon slice around 4-6 green beans.
5. Coat the pork tenderloins with oil.
6. After 15 minutes, add the pork tenderloins into the air fryer basket with potatoes and air fry for about 5-6 minutes.
7. Remove the pork tenderloins from the basket.
8. Place bean rolls into the basket and top with the pork tenderloins.
9. Air fry for another 7 minutes.
10. Remove from air fryer and transfer the pork tenderloins onto a platter.
11. Cut each tenderloin into desired size slices.
12. Serve alongside the potatoes and green beans rolls.

Nutrition:

- **Calories:** 918
- **Carbohydrate:** 42.4 g
- **Protein:** 77.9 g
- **Fat:** 47.7 g
- **Sugar:** 4 g
- **Sodium:** 1,400 mg

22. Pork Loin with Potatoes

Preparation Time: 15 minutes
Cooking Time: 25 minutes
Servings: 5
Ingredients:

- 2 lbs. pork loin
- 3 tbsps. olive oil, divided
- 1 tsp. fresh parsley, chopped
- Salt and ground black pepper, as required
- 3 large red potatoes, chopped
- ½ tsp. garlic powder
- ½ tsp. red pepper flakes, crushed

Directions:

1. Coat the pork loin with oil and then season evenly with parsley, salt, and black pepper.
2. In a large bowl, add the potatoes, remaining oil, garlic powder, red pepper flakes, salt, and black pepper and toss to coat well.
3. Set the temperature of the air fryer to 325°F. Grease an air fryer basket.
4. Place loin into the prepared air fryer basket.
5. Arrange potato pieces around the pork loin.
6. Air fry for about 25 minutes.
7. Remove from air fryer and transfer the pork loin onto a platter; wait for about 5 minutes before slicing.
8. Cut the pork loin into desired size slices and serve alongside the potatoes.

Nutrition:

- **Calories:** 556
- **Carbohydrate:** 29.6 g
- **Protein:** 44.9 g
- **Fat:** 28.3 g
- **Sugar:** 1.9 g
- **Sodium:** 132 mg

23. Pork Rolls

Preparation Time: 20 minutes
Cooking Time: 15 minutes
Servings: 4
Ingredients:

- 1 scallion, chopped
- ¼ cup sun-dried tomatoes, finely chopped
- 2 tbsps. fresh parsley, chopped
- Salt and ground black pepper, as required
- 4 6-oz. pork cutlets, pounded slightly
- 2 tsps. paprika
- ½ tbsp. olive oil

Directions:

1. In a bowl, mix well scallion, tomatoes, parsley, salt, and black pepper.
2. Spread the tomato mixture over each pork cutlet.
3. Roll each cutlet and secure it with cocktail sticks.
4. Rub the outer part of the rolls with paprika, salt, and black pepper.
5. Coat the rolls evenly with oil.
6. Set the temperature of the air fryer to 390°F. Grease an air fryer basket.
7. Arrange pork rolls into the prepared air fryer basket in a single layer.
8. Air fry for about 15 minutes.
9. Remove from air fryer and transfer the pork rolls onto serving plates.
10. Serve hot.

Nutrition:

- **Calories:** 244
- **Carbohydrate:** 14.5 g
- **Protein:** 20.1 g
- **Fat:** 8.2 g
- **Sugar:** 1.7 g
- **Sodium:** 708 mg

24. Pork Sausage Casserole

Preparation Time: 15 minutes
Cooking Time: 30 minutes
Servings: 4
Ingredients:

- 6 oz. flour, sifted
- 2 eggs
- 1 red onion, thinly sliced
- 1 garlic clove, minced
- Salt and ground black pepper, as required
- ¾ cup milk
- 2/3 cup cold water
- 8 small sausages
- 8 fresh rosemary sprigs

Directions:

1. In a bowl, mix together the flour and eggs.
2. Add the onion, garlic, salt, and black pepper. Mix them well.
3. Gently, add in the milk and water and mix until well combined.
4. In each sausage, pierce 1 rosemary sprig.
5. Set the temperature of the air fryer to 320°F. Grease a baking dish.
6. Arrange sausages into the prepared baking dish and top evenly with the flour mixture.
7. Air fry for about 30 minutes.
8. Remove from the air fryer and serve warm.

Nutrition:

- **Calories:** 334
- **Carbohydrate:** 37.7 g
- **Protein:** 14 g
- **Fat:** 14 g
- **Sugar:** 3.5 g
- **Sodium:** 250 mg

25. Rotisserie Chicken

Preparation Time: 10 minutes
Cooking Time: 30 minutes
Servings: 2
Ingredients:

- 1 whole chicken
- 2 tbsps. ghee
- 1 tbsp. magic mushroom powder
- Salt

Directions:

1. Preheat the Air Fryer to 370°F. Merge ghee and magic mushroom powder in a small mixing bowl.
2. Pull back the skin on the chicken breast and scoop some of the ghee mixtures between the breast and skin with a spoon.
3. Push the mixture with your fingers. Repeat this for the other breast. Season the chicken with salt.
4. Put the chicken breast-side down onto the wire basket. Cook at 365°F for about 30 minutes.
5. Serve.

Nutrition:

- **Calories:** 226
- **Carbs:** 0 g
- **Fat:** 14 g
- **Protein:** 44 g

26. Crispy Chicken Thighs

Preparation Time: 5 minutes
Cooking Time: 20 minutes
Servings: 2
Ingredients:

- 3 to 4 chicken thighs, skin on, bone removed, pat dry
- Salt
- Black pepper

Directions:

1. Preheat the Air Fryer to 400°F. Season the chicken with salt and pepper. Place the chicken in the Air Fryer basket.
2. Cook at 400°F for 18 minutes and top with black pepper.
3. Serve.

Nutrition:

- **Calories:** 104
- **Protein:** 13.5 g
- **Carbs:** 0 g
- **Fat:** 5.7 g

27. Chuck and Veggies

Preparation Time: 10 minutes
Cooking Time: 9 hours
Servings: 2
Ingredients:

- ¼ cup dry red wine
- ¼ tsp. salt
- 8 oz. boneless lean chuck roast
- ¼ tsp. black pepper
- 8 oz. frozen pepper stir-fry
- 1 tsp. Worcestershire sauce
- 8 oz. whole mushrooms
- 1 tsp. instant coffee granules
- 1 1/4 cups fresh green beans, trimmed
- 1 dried bay leaf

Directions:

1. Mix all the ingredients except salt in a bowl; combine well and then transfer to a slow cooker.
2. Cover the cooker and cook for about 9 hours on low and 4 1/2 hours on high, until beef is completely cooked through and tender.
3. Stir in ¼ tsp. salt gently. Take out the vegetables and beef and transfer to 2 shallow bowls.
4. Pour liquid into the skillet; boil it lightly and cook until liquid reduces to ¼ cup for about 1 1/2 minutes.
5. Pour over veggies and beef. Discard bay leaf and serve.

Nutrition:

- **Calories:** 215
- **Fat:** 5 g
- **Total carbs:** 17 g
- **Protein:** 26 g

28. Mustard Chicken with Basil

Preparation Time: 20 minutes
Cooking Time: 30 minutes
Servings: 4
Ingredients:

- 1 tsp. chicken stock
- 2 chicken breasts; skinless and boneless chicken breasts; halved
- 1 tbsp. chopped basil
- Salt and black pepper
- 1 tbsp. olive oil
- ½ tsp. garlic powder
- ½ tsp. onion powder
- 1 tsp. Dijon mustard

Directions:

1. Press 'Sauté' on the instant pot and add the oil. When it is hot, brown the chicken in it for 2–3 minutes.
2. Mix in the remaining ingredients and seal the lid to cook for 12 minutes at high pressure.
3. Natural release the pressure for 10 minutes, share into plates and serve.

Nutrition:

- **Calories:** 34
- **Fat:** 3.6 g
- **Carbs:** 0.7 g
- **Protein:** 0.3 g
- **Fiber:** 0.1 g

CHAPTER 5:

Desserts

1. Cinnamon Spiced Popcorn

Preparation Time: 10 minutes
Cooking Time: 5 minutes
Servings: 4
Ingredients:

- 8 cups air-popped corn
- 2 tsps. sugar
- ½ to 1 tsp. ground cinnamon
- Butter-flavored cooking spray

Directions:

1. Preheat the oven to 350°F and line a shallow roasting pan with foil.
2. Pop the popcorn using your preferred method.
3. Spread the popcorn in the roasting pan and mix the sugar and cinnamon in a small bowl.
4. Lightly spray the popcorn with cooking spray and toss to coat evenly.
5. Sprinkle with cinnamon and toss again.
6. Bake for 5 minutes until just crisp, then serve warm.

Nutrition:

- **Calories:** 70
- **Total fat:** 0.7 g
- **Saturated Fat:** 0.1 g
- **Total Carbs:** 14.7 g
- **Net Carbs:** 12.2 g
- **Protein:** 2.1 g
- **Sugar:** 2.2 g
- **Fiber:** 2.5 g
- **Sodium:** 1 mg

2.   Pumpkin Custard

Preparation Time: 2 hours 30 minutes
Cooking Time: 0 minutes
Servings: 6
Ingredients:

- 1/2 cup almond flour
- 4 eggs
- 1 cup pumpkin puree
- 1/2 cup stevia/erythritol blend, granulated
- 1/8 tsp. sea salt
- 1 tsp. vanilla extract or maple extract
- 4 tbsps. butter, ghee, or coconut oil melted
- 1 tsp. pumpkin pie spice
- Stevie-sweetened whipped cream (optional, for serving)
- Nutmeg (optional, for serving)

Directions:

1. Grease or spray a slow cooker with butter or coconut oil.
2. In a medium mixing bowl, beat the eggs until smooth. Then add in the sweetener.
3. To the egg mixture, add in the pumpkin puree along with vanilla or maple extract.
4. Then add almond flour to the mixture along with the pumpkin pie spice and salt. Add melted butter, coconut oil, or ghee.
5. Set slow cooker to the low setting. Cook for 2–2.45 hours, and begin checking at the two-hour mark. Serve warm with stevia-sweetened whipped cream and a sprinkle of nutmeg.

Nutrition:

- **Calories:** 70
- **Total fat:** 0.7 g
- **Saturated Fat:** 0.1 g
- **Total Carbs:** 14.7 g
- **Net Carbs:** 12.2 g
- **Protein:** 2.1 g
- **Sugar:** 2.2 g
- **Fiber:** 2.5 g
- **Sodium:** 1 mg

3.   Peanut Butter Banana "Ice Cream"

Preparation Time: 10 minutes
Cooking Time: 0 minutes
Servings: 6
Ingredients:

- 4 medium bananas
- ½ cup whipped peanut butter
- 1 tsp. vanilla extract

Directions:

1. Peel the bananas and slice them into coins.
2. Arrange the slices on a plate and freeze until solid.
3. Place the frozen bananas in a food processor.
4. Add the peanut butter and blend until it is mostly smooth.
5. Scrape down the sides, then add the vanilla extract.
6. Pulse until smooth, then spoon into bowls to serve.

Nutrition:

- **Calories:** 70
- **Total fat:** 0.7 g
- **Saturated Fat:** 0.1 g
- **Total Carbs:** 14.7 g
- **Net Carbs:** 12.2 g
- **Protein:** 2.1 g
- **Sugar:** 2.2 g
- **Fiber:** 2.5 g
- **Sodium:** 1 mg

4. Fruity Coconut Energy Balls

Preparation Time: 15 minutes
Cooking Time: 0 minutes
Servings: 18
Ingredients:

- 1 cup chopped almonds
- 1 cup dried figs
- ½ cup dried apricots, chopped
- ½ cup dried cranberries, unsweetened
- ½ tsp. vanilla extract
- ¼ tsp. ground cinnamon
- ½ cup shredded unsweetened coconut

Directions:

1. Place the almonds, figs, apricots, and cranberries in a food processor.
2. Pulse the mixture until finely chopped.
3. Add the vanilla extract and cinnamon, then pulse to blend once more.
4. Roll the mixture into 18 small balls by hand.
5. Roll the balls in the shredded coconut and chill until firm.

Nutrition:

- **Calories:** 100
- **Total fat:** 0.7 g
- **Saturated Fat:** 0.1 g
- **Total Carbs:** 14.7 g
- **Net Carbs:** 12.2 g
- **Protein:** 2.1 g
- **Sugar:** 2.2 g
- **Fiber:** 2.5 g
- **Sodium:** 1 mg

5. Date Haroset

Preparation Time: 45 minutes
Cooking Time: 1 hour
Servings: 40
Ingredients:

- 1/2 lb. chopped dates
- 1 cup golden raisins
- 1/2 cup red wine
- 1/2 cup coarsely chopped walnuts
- 1 tsp. ground cinnamon
- 1/2 cup confectioners' sugar

Directions:

1. In a small saucepan with the wine, put golden raisins and chopped dates. Let it cook on low heat, stirring from time to time until the fruit thickens and forms a soft paste. Allow it to cool.
2. Stir the cinnamon and nuts into the cooled fruit mixture.
3. Shape the paste into small, bite-sized balls, then roll it in confectioner's sugar.

Nutrition:

- **Calories:** 47
- **Total Carbohydrate:** 9.4 g
- **Cholesterol:** 0 mg
- **Protein:** 0.5 g
- **Total fat:** 1 g
- **Sodium:** 1 mg

6. Dolce Pesca (Sweet Peaches)

Preparation Time: 15 minutes
Cooking Time: 15 minutes
Servings: 8
Ingredients:

- 4 fresh figs
- 1/2 cup pine nuts
- 4 peaches, halved and pitted
- 1/4 cup white sugar
- 1 cup white wine
- 1/2 cup brandy

Directions:

1. Preheat oven to 190°C/375°F. Line foil on a baking sheet.
2. In a food processor bowl, pulse pine nuts and figs until fine. Put halved peaches, cut side up, on prepped baking sheet. Evenly sprinkle white sugar. Put white wine on peaches. Stuff them using the fig mixture. Put brandy on peaches.
3. In the preheated oven, bake for 15 minutes until browned.

Nutrition:

- **Calories:** 172
- **Total fat:** 4.4 g
- **Sodium:** 4 mg
- **Total Carbohydrate:** 16.1 g
- **Cholesterol:** 0 mg
- **Protein:** 2.3 g

7.   Fresh Strawberry Granita

Preparation Time: 10 minutes
Cooking Time: 0 minutes
Servings: 8
Ingredients:

- 2 pounds ripe strawberries, hulled and halved
- 1/3 cup white sugar, or to taste
- 1 cup water
- 1/2 tsp. lemon juice (optional)
- 1/4 tsp. balsamic vinegar (optional)
- 1 tiny pinch of salt

Directions:

1. With cold water, rinse strawberries; let them drain. Put berries into a blender; add salt, balsamic vinegar, lemon juice, water, and sugar.
2. Pulse the mixture several times to get it moving, then blend for about 1 minute until smooth. Transfer to a large baking dish. Puree should be only about 3/8 inch deep in the dish.
3. Put the dish without a cover in the freezer for about 45 minutes until the mixture barely starts to freeze around the edges. Its center will be slushy.
4. Stir the crystals lightly with a fork from the edge of the granita mixture into the center; mix thoroughly. Close the freezer; chill for 30–40 minutes more until granita becomes nearly frozen. Using a fork, mix lightly as before, scraping the crystals loose. Freeze again and stir 3–4 times with a fork until the granita becomes light, looks fluffy and dry, and crystals are separate.
5. Divide granita into small serving bowls; serve.

Nutrition:

- **Calories:** 69
- **Total fat:** 0.3 g
- **Sodium:** 26 mg
- **Total Carbohydrate:** 17.1 g
- **Cholesterol:** 0 mg
- **Protein:** 0.8 g

8.   Fruit Bake

Preparation Time: 20 minutes
Cooking Time: 35 minutes
Servings: 8
Ingredients:

- 6 fresh peaches, pitted and chopped
- 2 pears, peeled, cored, and chopped
- 4 stalks rhubarb, cut into ½-inch pieces
- 2 tbsps. raisins
- 1 large papaya, peeled, seeded, and cubed (optional)
- 2 tbsps. biscuit baking mix
- 1/4 cup light brown sugar
- 1 tbsp. margarine, softened

Directions:

1. Set an oven to preheat to 190°C (375°F), then grease a 9x13-inch baking dish.
2. In the prepped pan, lay out the papaya, raisins, rhubarb, pears, and peaches. Mix together the margarine, brown sugar, and baking mix in a medium bowl, then mix until the mixture has a crumbly texture. Evenly sprinkle on top of the fruit.
3. Let it bake in the preheated oven for 35–45 minutes until the top becomes golden brown.

Nutrition:

- **Calories:** 93
- **Cholesterol:** 0 mg
- **Protein:** 0.8 g
- **Total fat:** 1.8 g
- **Sodium:** 44 mg
- **Total Carbohydrate:** 20 g

9.   Healthy and Tasty Strawberry Sherbet

Preparation Time: 5 minutes
Cooking Time: 0 minutes
Servings: 4
Ingredients:

- 2 cups frozen strawberries
- 2 tbsps. white sugar
- 1 tsp. lemon juice

Directions:

1. In a food processor, put strawberries and beat about 30 seconds until smooth. Beat in lemon juice and sugar, about 10 seconds more.
2. Put sherbet in the freezer for about 1 hour until solid.

Nutrition:

- **Calories:** 63
- **Total fat:** 0.1 g
- **Sodium:** 2 mg
- **Total Carbohydrate:** 16.5 g
- **Cholesterol:** 0 mg
- **Protein:** 0.5 g

10. Kabocha Squash Pie (Japanese Pumpkin Pie)

Preparation Time: 20 minutes
Cooking Time: 35 minutes
Servings: 8
Ingredients:
Crust:

- 3/4 cup graham crackers, crushed
- 1/2 cup all-purpose flour
- 1/8 cup light soy butter
- 1 tbsp. soy milk

Filling:

- 2 1/3 cups kabocha squash, halved, peeled, seeded, and cut into 1 ½-inch cubes
- 2/3 cup silken tofu
- 1 tsp. vanilla extract
- 1/4 cup white sugar
- 1/2 tsp. ground cinnamon
- 1/4 tsp. ground nutmeg

Directions:

1. Preheat an oven to 175°C/350°F.
2. In a mixing bowl, mix flour and graham cracker crumbs; mix in soy butter until it is crumbly. Create a well in the center of the flour mixture. Add soy milk; mix to make a soft dough. Turn out dough on a lightly floured surface; briefly knead. In a plastic wrap, wrap; refrigerate for 20 minutes.
3. Roll dough out to 1/4-in. thick on a lightly floured surface. Fit pie crust in a 7-in. diameter pie plate; poke holes in the bottom with a fork.
4. In the preheated oven, bake the crust for 15 minutes until pale golden; on the rack, cool.
5. Put 1-in. water on the bottom of the pan. Put kabocha in a steamer basket fitted into pan; boil. Lower heat to medium and cover; steam squash for 15 minutes until easily pierced with fork and tender. Cool.
6. Blend kabocha till smooth in a food processor's bowl/blender. Mix nutmeg, cinnamon, sugar, vanilla, and tofu into kabocha mixture; blend until very smooth. Put into prepped crust.
7. In the preheated oven, bake for 20 minutes until the middle is set; don't overbake; filling will crack.

Nutrition:

- **Calories:** 137 **Sodium:** 65 mg
- **Total Carbohydrate:** 23.1 g **Cholesterol:** 1
- **Protein:** 4.2 g **Total fat:** 3.3 g

11. Mini Apple Oat Muffins

Preparation Time: 5minutes
Cooking Time: 25 minutes
Servings: 24
Ingredients:

- 1 ½ cups old-fashioned oats
- 1 tsp. baking powder
- ½ tsp. ground cinnamon
- ¼ tsp. baking soda
- ¼ tsp. salt
- ½ cup unsweetened applesauce
- ¼ cup light brown sugar
- 3 tbsps. canola oil
- 3 tbsps. water
- 1 tsp. vanilla extract
- ½ cup slivered almonds

Directions:

1. Preheat the oven to 350°F and grease a mini muffin pan.
2. Place the oats in a food processor and pulse into a fine flour.
3. Add the baking powder, cinnamon, baking soda, and salt.
4. Pulse until well combined, then add the applesauce, brown sugar, canola oil, water, and vanilla, then blend smooth.
5. Fold in the almonds and spoon the mixture into the muffin pan.
6. Bake for 22 to 25 minutes until a knife inserted in the center comes out clean.
7. Cool the muffins for 5 minutes, then turn them out onto a wire rack.

Nutrition:

- **Calories:** 70
- **Total fat:** 0.7 g
- **Saturated Fat:** 0.1 g
- **Total Carbs:** 14.7 g
- **Net Carbs:** 12.2 g
- **Protein:** 2.1 g
- **Sugar:** 2.2 g
- **Fiber:** 2.5 g
- **Sodium:** 1 mg

12. Dark Chocolate Almond Yogurt Cups

Preparation Time: 10 minutes
Cooking Time: 0 minutes
Servings: 6
Ingredients:

- 3 cups plain non-fat Greek yogurt
- ½ tsp. almond extract
- ¼ tsp. liquid stevia extract (more to taste)
- 2 oz. 70% dark chocolate, chopped
- ½ cup slivered almonds

Directions:

1. Whisk together the yogurt, almond extract, and liquid stevia in a medium bowl.
2. Spoon the yogurt into four dessert cups.
3. Sprinkle with chopped chocolate and slivered almonds.

Nutrition:

- **Calories:** 170
- **Total fat:** 0.7 g
- **Saturated Fat:** 0.1 g
- **Total Carbs:** 14.7 g
- **Net Carbs:** 12.2 g
- **Protein:** 2.1 g
- **Sugar:** 2.2 g
- **Fiber:** 2.5 g
- **Sodium:** 41 mg

13. Chocolate Avocado Mousse

Preparation Time: 5 minutes
Cooking Time: 0 minutes
Servings: 3
Ingredients:

- 1 large avocado, pitted and chopped
- ¼ cup fat-free milk
- ¼ cup unsweetened cocoa powder (dark)
- 2 tsps. powdered stevia
- 1 tsp. vanilla extract
- 2 tbsps. fat-free whipped topping

Directions:

1. Place the avocado in a food processor and blend until smooth.
2. In a small bowl, whisk together the milk and cocoa powder until well combined.
3. Stir in the pureed avocado along with the stevia and vanilla extract.
4. Spoon into bowls and serve with fat-free whipped topping.

Nutrition:

- **Calories:** 180
- **Total fat:** 0.7 g
- **Saturated Fat:** 0.1 g
- **Total Carbs:** 14.7 g
- **Net Carbs:** 12.2 g
- **Protein:** 2.1 g
- **Sugar:** 2.2 g
- **Fiber:** 2.5 g
- **Sodium:** 23 mg

14. Pumpkin Spice Snack Balls

Preparation Time: 15 minutes
Cooking Time: 10 minutes
Servings: 10
Ingredients:

- 1 ½ cups old-fashioned oats
- ½ cup chopped almonds
- ½ cup unsweetened shredded coconut
- ¾ cup canned pumpkin puree
- 2 tbsps. honey
- 2 tsps. pumpkin pie spice
- ¼ tsp. salt

Directions:

1. Preheat the oven to 300°F and line a baking sheet with parchment.
2. Combine the oats, almonds, and coconut on the baking sheet.
3. Bake for 8 to 10 minutes until browned, stirring halfway through.
4. Place the pumpkin, honey, pumpkin pie spice, and salt in a medium bowl.
5. Stir in the toasted oat mixture.
6. Shape the mixture into 20 balls by hand and place on a tray.
7. Chill until the balls are firm, then serve.

Nutrition:

- **Calories:** 170
- **Total fat:** 0.7 g
- **Saturated Fat:** 0.1 g
- **Total Carbs:** 14.7 g
- **Net Carbs:** 12.2 g
- **Protein:** 2.1 g
- **Sugar:** 2.2 g
- **Fiber:** 2.5 g
- **Sodium:** 1 mg

15. Strawberry-Lime Pudding

Preparation Time: 15 minutes
Cooking Time: 10 minutes
Servings: 4
Ingredients:

- 2 cups + 2 tbsps. fat-free milk
- 2 tsps. flavorless gelatin
- 10 large strawberries, sliced
- 1 tbsp. fresh lime zest
- 2 tsps. vanilla extract
- Liquid stevia extract, to taste
- 2 tbsp. lime juice

Directions:

1. Whisk together 2 tbsps. milk and gelatin in a medium bowl until the gelatin dissolves completely.
2. Place the strawberries in a food processor with lime juice and vanilla extract.
3. Blend until smooth, then pour into a medium bowl.
4. Warm the remaining milk in a small saucepan over medium heat.
5. Stir in the lime zest and heat until steaming (do not boil).
6. Gently whisk the gelatin mixture into the hot milk, then stir in the strawberry mixture.
7. Sweeten with liquid stevia to taste and chill until set. Serve cold.

Nutrition:

- **Calories:** 70
- **Total fat:** 0.7 g
- **Saturated Fat:** 0.1 g
- **Total Carbs:** 14.7 g
- **Net Carbs:** 12.2 g
- **Protein:** 2.1 g
- **Sugar:** 2.2 g
- **Fiber:** 2.5 g
- **Sodium:** 1 mg

Conclusion

And there you have it! Diabetic meal planning and prepping doesn't need to be difficult. You just prep ahead of time—and when you do that, you will have all the foods exactly how you need them. This meal plan recommended to you is just one of many—you can create your own with your own preferences, the season, and what you happen to have one hand at the time that you are ready to eat.

When it comes to enjoying the recipes in this book, you will be nourishing your body in a healthy way, even though the foods are as good as they are. You will also be setting up with planning that you can use to avoid the confusion of trying to make your meals on the spot and realizing that you are out of ingredients. It takes the complication out of eating, and that can be a huge blessing in such a busy time as these days.

Thank you for picking up this book to use as your guide to meal planning, prepping, and recipes that you can learn to enjoy at home without worrying about what is in them. Hopefully, as you read through this book, you gained all sorts of valuable knowledge, and you feel confident in the ability to make sure that you are enjoying nourishing yourself!

Finally, if you found this book useful in any way, a review on Amazon is always appreciated! Let us know what your favorite recipe was, or provide any feedback for how you felt this book handled these recipes. Good luck and happy eating!

Made in the USA
Monee, IL
11 October 2021